COPPERCRAFT
and SILVER
MADE AT HOME

COPPERCRAFT and SILVER MADE AT HOME

by Karl Robert Kramer and Nora Kramer

Drawings by Joan Stoliar

Photographs by Keith B. Norris

DOVER PUBLICATIONS, INC.
NEW YORK

This Dover edition, first published in 1972, is an
unabridged republication of the work originally
published by Greenberg Publisher, New York, in
1957.
The list of Sources of Supply (page 175) has been
revised for the present edition.

International Standard Book Number: 0-486-22790-1
Library of Congress Catalog Card Number: 70-178088

Manufactured in the United States of America
Dover Publications, Inc.
180 Varick Street
New York, N. Y. 10014

For Miriam and Ruth

Acknowledgments

In a book of this sort, in which details of familiar activities often take longer in the telling than in actual doing, the authors are particularly indebted to those whose patience and industry were closely associated with its development.

To Ruth Kramer, whose steady service included not only preparing the manuscript, but many practical and illuminating suggestions; to Miriam Phillips, listener par excellence, whose orderly thinking, critical ear, and constructive advice brought stimulus and assurance throughout; to the family of craftsmen, who for holiday weekends, turned into a reading circle and a discussion group, invaluable in its searching comment; to Arthur Stoliar, whose perceptive criticism and lively memories of early craft experiences strengthened the authors' feeling for the reader's needs; to Joan Stoliar, for her sound evaluation of presentation and expert correlation of detail, as well as for her illuminative illustrations; to old friends May and Mickey Oren and Fannie Gittleman, who by their magic, in relays, multiplied the hours of many days when hours were needed, yet helped to make them fly; and to all those friends, who over the years asked for details of construction of objects they admired in the homes of the authors. By their questions they kept alive the idea of a book of usable crafts by experienced craftsmen for beginning amateurs. To all of these, many thanks indeed.

Karl Robert Kramer
Nora Kramer

Contents

COPPERCRAFT
and SILVER
MADE AT HOME

Chapter I

GETTING STARTED

THERE IS DEEP SATISFACTION IN LOOKING ABOUT YOUR HOME AT HANDSOME decorative objects you have made yourself. There is even greater satisfaction in using them and in receiving the praise and admiration of others for your skill.

Being able at will to design and create a thing of beauty for personal pleasure or for a gift to fill a social need, brings a gratifying sense of power and accomplishment. Most rewarding of all is the knowledge that the creation of each object opens a door to the making of other things in a variety that is literally endless.

For the beginning amateur with limited leisure and no particular artistic training, metalcraft is an excellent choice as a creative hobby. Other media may seem less forbidding than metal, but the truth is that silver and copper are more easily worked at home than many other materials. The mistaken belief that working in metals requires a "real" workshop has denied a rich experience to many a would-be craftsman.

Actual procedures as given in each of the following projects are simple, and the directions offered are precise; so that each of the copper and silver objects presented here will be beautiful, even when made for the first time by a person with no previous experience. These projects have actually been made in ordinary home kitchens, with simple equipment, by amateurs of all ages. These people had no previous training and were not "gifted" except in a few instances. At camp, children and young people of ten to seventeen years made many variations of these projects, though their previous craft experience had been limited to the average minor crafts usually done at camp.

The campers used the same simple processes used by the kitchen crafts-men, and presented here. Each was encouraged to "work large" wherever possible; to follow mechanical procedures exactly as prescribed, but to follow his own creative ideas in carefully planning the design. As a result, they made trays, plates, and jewelry of such beauty that each thoroughly respected himself for his achievement and treasured what he had made. He had the satisfaction of knowing that he had done every step himself.

When camp closed for the summer, it was both amusing and touching to see the practically indestructible copper plate carried home by hand, lest "something happen to it" if entrusted to the home-going trunk.

Design is where you find it; you learn to look with a fresh eye at familiar things about you. Once you discover that the pleasing motif on the wall paper in the hall might make a fine center for a large plate, you begin to realize that an idea can come from anywhere. A casual unit from the rug, the attractive photograph frame in a magazine, or the sketched border from a newspaper advertisement can become for you the nucleus of a basic decoration. You learn to develop these ideas into forms of your own with initial courage and increasing assurance.

HOW TO DEVELOP YOUR OWN DESIGNS

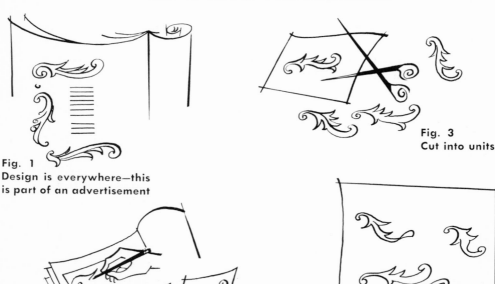

Fig. 1
Design is everywhere—this
is part of an advertisement

Fig. 3
Cut into units

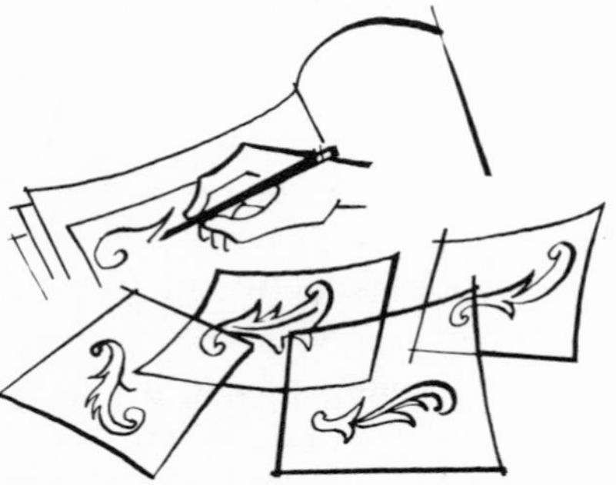

Fig. 2
Make several tracings of
pleasing unit

Fig. 4
Try many arrangements of
units on tracing paper cut
to size of project

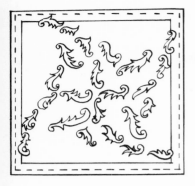

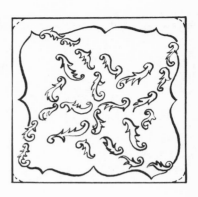

Fig. 5
Experimenting with straight borders

Fig. 6
Final choice of curved border

The design of the square 12-inch plate in Chapter 11 was developed by a teen-ager from two single units cut from the border around a magazine advertisement. She traced and cut many copies of the unit and moved them about on a 12-inch square of white paper that represented her plate, until she evolved a pleasing design. (See Figs. 1, 2, 3, 4.) At first she tried a narrow straight border for her design, then straight borders of varying widths, but none was suitable. When she tried the Ess *curve* she knew instantly it was "right." (See Figs. 5 and 6.)

This method is possible for anyone. It acts as a release to those who feel that they are not artistic because they "can't even draw a straight line!" That poor straight line! Its valid place in geometry and elsewhere is not disputed, but its power as a measure of artistic ability has been greatly overrated.

The truth is that a great deal of latent ability is never discovered except by accident. Often it takes an unusual combination of circumstances to shake a person out of his humility concerning his capabilities. The individual who does not hesitate to trust his taste in clothes, in his work, in his home, will often be surprised to learn that *good taste* is artistry! Good taste stems from the same source which in some people results in painting or drawing, in the fine piece of sculpture, the beautifully designed jewelled object—all, in fact, of the myriad beauties that are found in art and in crafts.

A woman who once thought of herself as anything but creative found that the years spent in the park with her small children had left her with a memory for bird poses she hadn't known she possessed. She couldn't draw, but when she tried ceramic clay, she found it a happy medium for her. The birds she modeled had character and charm, and she had a hobby that enriched the years after her children were grown.

A man who read about metalcraft courses with real longing waited for years without being able to arrange for regular leisure in which to take them. Then he discovered he could work at home in the scattered leisure that was his, with gratifying results.

Metalcraft courses are given in many craft centers and schools, but it takes time and effort to attend, and the hours are not always convenient.

Fig. 7
Planning

Fortunately you can learn metalry in copper and silver at home, and work in your own time, at your own pace. It is wonderful to have at hand a project that you can pick up at any time to fill odd moments of leisure— a project that will not suffer damage by being left for uncertain periods. This freedom of action will be reflected in the freshness and spontaneity of your work and your constant enjoyment of it.

Before we discuss the arrangement of working space, you would probably like a quick preview of what is actually involved in the projects in this book. The process is approximately the same for silver or copper. The general stages are: *planning, cutting* (in some cases), *beveling, tracing, scribing, etching,* and *shaping your piece.*

We have already discussed the planning of designs to some extent, and the directions for each project go into more specific detail.

In many of the projects, you start with a piece of copper which is purchased already cut to the desired size and shape. In others, you do the cutting yourself. Next, you bevel and smooth the edges of the piece.

Then you transfer your design from paper to the piece by means of carbon paper, and you "scribe" or incise the design lightly onto the metal.

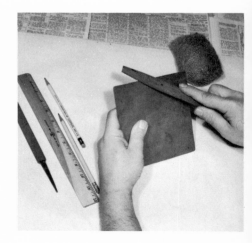

Fig. 8
Cutting

Fig. 9
Beveling

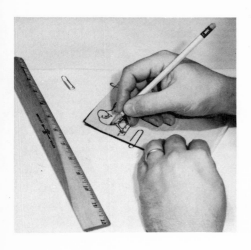

Fig. 10
Tracing

Fig. 11
Scribing

The etching is done with a corrosive acid which literally eats away parts of the metal. This is accomplished by painting the parts of the design that are to remain *unetched* with a protective coating of "asphaltum," a substance which is impervious to acid. The object is then given a timed acid bath, washed, and the asphaltum coating removed.

Finally, you hammer the piece into the desired shape, sometimes by means of a wooden mold. Then you antique it and polish it.

You will learn exactly how to go about each separate action in easy, step-by-step stages.

Your kitchen, as it stands, offers facilities for these operations. The kitchen table—or a counter top or card table—can be used for designing, scribing, and painting with asphaltum. Thick newspapers should be spread over the entire table surface before you begin operations. This simple precaution not only protects the furniture, but releases you from anxieties that would divide your attention.

Fig. 12
Etching

Fig. 13
Shaping

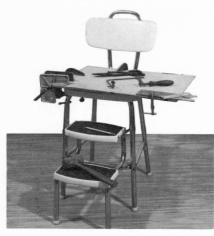

Fig. 14
Kitchen stool into workbench

When it is necessary to flatten a piece of metal with a buckskin mallet, the floor does very well. For other operations you can make an effective workbench from your kitchen stepstool. (If you do not own one, we recommend it as a worthwhile purchase for domestic as well as craft purposes!)

To convert your stool to a workbench, clamp a board approximately 22 x 15 x ⅜ inches firmly to the seat by two C clamps, size 5 (see Fig. 14). To this board you can clamp, as you need it, either a V board (used in cutting silver) or a small vise. If necessary, you can use this as a stand for the etching bin, as it is easily moved to any spot that is convenient and safe during the etching process.

Pulling out the stool steps provides several handy resting places for tools, and you can work from either side, depending on whether you are right-handed or left-handed.

These adjustments make a surprisingly efficient workshop of your kitchen; yet it takes but a very few moments to remove all trace of them and restore the kitchen to its normal uses.

Each project in this book prepares you for the next in skill as well as materials. The equipment for the first project fills your *basic* needs, and you will use this same equipment again and again. For later projects there are occasional additions, so that your assortment of tools will keep pace with your growing skill. Every project is planned to achieve maximum results in terms of beauty and utility, with a minimum of effort and financial outlay.

You can purchase all materials at handicraft supply stores or by mail order. (See listing in Appendix.) As already mentioned, you can buy copper in squares and circles of the desired size, and in the gauge suggested for the project. You can effect a saving by buying larger sheets of the same gauge and cutting out the shapes yourself, and for some of the later projects this will be necessary. However, for these first projects we suggest that you buy ready-made sizes.

For the projects in silver, you buy the silver in the gauge you need and overall size that you estimate is needed for one or more projects, and cut the shapes at home.

And now to begin!

Chapter 2

SQUARE TEA PLATE IN COPPER

HERE ARE THE MATERIALS YOU WILL NEED TO BEGIN THIS PROJECT. ON THE left are those you will probably have to purchase (and you will use the tools for all the copper projects in the book). On the right are those items which are likely to be on hand and need only to be assembled.

1 6-inch square of copper, 18-gauge
1 half-round metal file (in purchasing, ask for "single cut, second cut")
1 flat metal file (in purchasing, ask for "single cut fine")
1 package 1/0 steel wool
1 scriber or sharp awl
1 paint brush, size 5

1 pint jar of white tempera (water color poster paint—a pint is enough for several projects)
1 sheet carbon paper
1 sharp pencil #2
scissors
paper clips
old newspapers
tracing paper

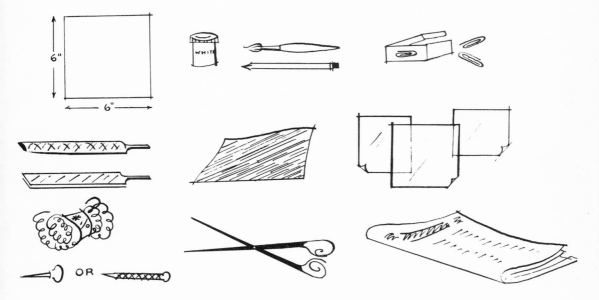

Fig. 15
Cutting copper to size

Step 1—Beveling Metal Edges

You have your ready-cut square of copper (or you will cut it from a larger piece—see Fig. 15), and all its edges are sharp. Your first step is to transform the square edges into a rounded bevel with a smooth satiny feel. This is done by alternately filing the edges with the metal files and rubbing with steel wool.

Hold the copper upright in one hand and the flat side of the coarser, half-round file at an angle of 45° in the other. File up and over, up and over, along the entire edge, to keep an even line to the bevel. (See Figs. 16 and 17.) Turn the copper over from time to time so that you work from both sides. Round the four corners of the square slightly, just enough to remove the sharp point. (See Fig. 18.) Rub with steel wool frequently and test the smoothness of the bevel by rubbing your fingers carefully along the edges. (See Fig. 19.) When the sharp edges are gone, finish the beveling with the finer file, alternating with the steel wool. (See Fig. 20.)

This is not difficult and does not take long, but if you learn to finish the metal edges quickly and well, it will help you in every project in the book.

Fig. 16
Beveling—proper position of file to begin stroke

Fig. 17
Beveling position when completing stroke

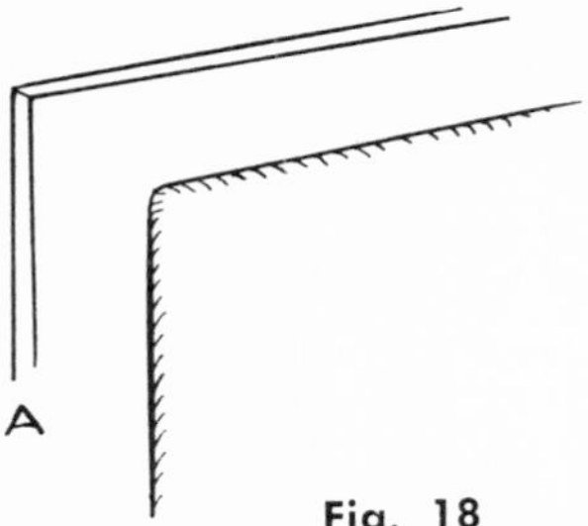

Fig. 19
Alternate rubbing with steel wool shortens beveling time

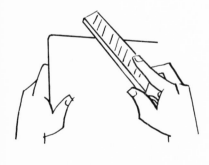

A

B

Fig. 18
Round corners slightly with file

Step 2—The Design

Always start by cutting the sheet of tracing paper, on which you will work your design, to the exact size of your project. You will find that it will simplify the placement of your design when you are ready to transfer it to the copper.

Place the beveled copper on a sheet of tracing paper, mark around it accurately in pencil, and cut out the square of paper to use as your design sheet. (See Fig. 21.) (A firm tracing paper such as is used by architects is best; it can be bought by the yard in artist's supply stores, but any firm clear quality of tracing paper will do.) Cut a piece of carbon paper to the same size and set it aside for the moment.

Fig. 21
Cut tracing paper to size of project

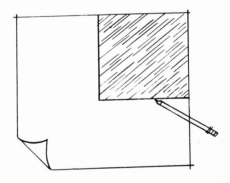

Fig. 20
Lightly finish with finer (flat) file

Fig. 22
Tracing design from source

Step 3

Let us say that you are taking as your design part of the motif in a magazine advertisement. Lay your square of tracing paper on the magazine page, move it about until the placement of the design pleases you, then trace it. (See Fig. 22.) Remember in placing the design that there will be a center depression 3 inches in diameter on the finished tea plate, and allow for it.

Study the traced design. If the result is not as pleasing as you thought it would be, feel free to make changes—to add to it and to experiment. Cut out several squares of paper the size of your copper and try out variations in the design. Cut the design into small pieces and put it together differently, moving it about on the square of tracing paper. When it pleases you, paste the pieces down, in the design you have made, on the tracing paper. Outline your design heavily in pencil so you can later trace it onto a fresh piece of tracing paper.

The time you spend experimenting with design will not be wasted; it will help you to gain in judgment and in assurance as you progress, so that your freedom to create, to find, and to adapt design will keep pace with your mastery of technical procedures. You will discover that this is an important gain for a craftsman.

Now that your design is worked out, lay over it a fresh piece of tracing paper, cut to the size of the copper, and trace a careful, clean copy with a sharp pencil. Have your design very clean and clear before attempting to transfer it to the metal.

Fig. 23
Exact size for tracing

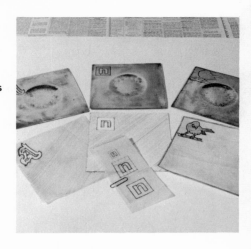

Fig. 24
Three designs—three borders

If you wish to use the bird design we have used, trace it from Fig. 23.

A design sheet must *always* include a border. This border, around the design, or around the edge of the plate, is later painted with acid-resistant asphaltum to project the edges of each project from the acid; it *must* be indicated in the design. (See comparison in Fig. 24. Note that the bird design plate has a narrow border on the edge, while the two designs of initials carry their own borders.)

Step 4—Transferring the Design

Clean your copper square thoroughly with steel wool. Examine it for flaws—slight scratches or other markings. Most copper cut pieces have one side that is slightly better than the other; choose this side for the side to which you will transfer your design.

Lay the cleaned copper face-up on a newspaper-covered table, being careful to avoid fingerprints on the cleaned surface. Paint the surface with a thin layer of white tempera and allow it to dry. (See Fig. 25.) If the paint "crawls"—that is, shrinks away from the area instead of covering it—it means the copper is not clean enough. Wash off the paint, dry the plate thoroughly, and clean it again with steel wool. Hold it by the edges with a clean cloth or paper. Repaint with the tempera. If the copper is really clean, the paint will spread evenly and dry to a good working surface.

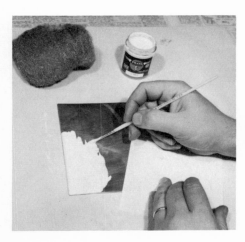

Fig. 25
Painting cleaned copper
with white tempera

Fig. 26
Design over carbon paper
on white-painted copper

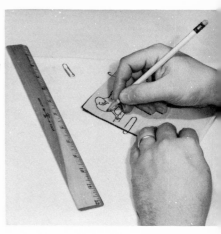

Fig. 27
Trace the design with sharp
pencil

Step 5

Now lay the square of carbon paper, carbon-side down, over the dry white surface; over that lay the clear design on the square of tracing paper. (See Fig. 26.) Line up all edges and secure them all around with paper clips. Two on each side will do. With a sharp pencil carefully trace your design. (See Fig. 27.) After tracing, leave one corner well anchored by the clips, and lift the rest to check. (See Fig. 28.) In this way, if any lines have been omitted, it is easy to drop your design back on the exact spot and fill in the omissions. Use a ruler to guide your pencil when transferring the border lines. (See Fig. 29.) Now lift the papers off the copper without smudging the carbon. If the design is clearly outlined, you are ready to scribe the design into the copper.

Step 6

Your scriber is a sharp-pointed tool or a sharpened awl. With the scriber outline the design along the carbon line firmly enough to penetrate the white paint and leave a strong design on the copper. But do not press so hard that you cannot turn the scriber with ease on the curves of the design. (See Fig. 30.) When you have finished scribing the design, wash off the white paint. (See Fig. 31.) Your plate must now be cleaned thoroughly on both sides to prepare it for the next step. This is painting the plate with asphaltum to prepare it for the etching process.

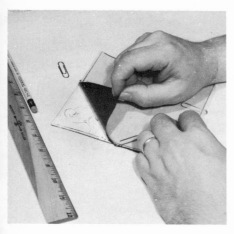

Fig. 28
Check to see all lines are
traced

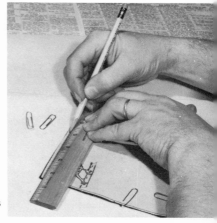

Fig. 29
Use ruler to transfer borders

Fig. 30
Scribing design on copper

Fig. 31
Washing white paint from
scribed Copper Plate

Step 7

You will now need the following materials:

1 artist's brush #1–#3
1 artist's brush #4–#5
1 pt. can asphaltum (will be used for several projects)
1 qt. turpentine
1 lb. nitric acid, concentrated,
    or
1 lb. etching mordant for copper (in chunks)
    or
1 qt. etching mordant for copper (liquid, ready to use)
    an old spoon (a plastic spoon will do)

1 glass dish or *unchipped* enamel basin (for rinsing)
    newsprint (bought in a pad)
1 glass measuring cup
1 glass dish at least 8 inches in diameter (for etching bin)
2 wooden clothespins—no metal
1 discarded pie plate (for turpentine rinse)
    soft rags and a small jar with a screw top
1 extra glass bottle with glass stopper (for used nitric acid solution)

Gather the materials you need for immediate use—brushes, asphaltum, turpentine, rags, small low jar with a screw top, your scribed copper square and steel wool to keep it clean, and pad of newsprint. Now you are ready to prepare your plate for etching by painting the design, the border, and the back of the plate with an acid resist. We use asphaltum, which is a black varnish that is not affected by acid or other etching agents.

Generally, asphaltum is of a good painting texture when the can is first opened. It can be thinned with turpentine from time to time to maintain the proper consistency. However, a good working method which prevents unnecessary thickening is to use the original can as a source of supply instead of working directly from it. For each project, transfer a small amount of asphaltum into a small jar with a cover that can be screwed on between working sessions. In that way you can keep the original can tightly closed most of the time, and the asphaltum remains at the texture of medium-thick cream or nail polish and will spread easily. It is better to use an old spoon or small ladle to fill the jar, as pouring leaves a deposit on the edge of the can.

Fig. 32
Turning scribed side down
on newsprint

Fig. 33
Painting well-cleaned back
of Copper Plate

Step 8—Painting with Asphaltum

Lay your thoroughly clean plate on a sheet of newsprint, *with the scribed side down*. (See Fig. 32.) Avoid fingerprints on the copper, as oils in the skin prevent the asphaltum from taking hold. Another caution: do not make the mistake of substituting newspaper for blank newsprint. Printer's ink on newspaper combines with the materials used in painting and etching to make almost indelible stains on the copper. Newsprint is the blank paper used for newspapers. It comes in pads at stationers and craft supply houses.

Using the thicker brush, paint the back (that is, the unscribed side) of your plate with asphaltum, covering the entire surface, and making sure that you carry the asphaltum to the very edge of the copper. (See Fig. 33.) Examine your work for spots that look reddish—in those spots the asphaltum is too thin. Paint these parts over. Without waiting for the asphaltum to dry, lay over it a double thickness of newsprint about 12 inches in diameter. (See Fig. 34.) The wet surface will stick to the paper, and you can then turn the plate over onto the double thickness of newsprint. (See Fig. 35.)

Fig. 34
Covering wet asphaltum
with double newsprint

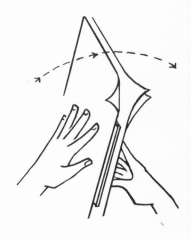

Fig. 35
Turning Plate over on
double newsprint

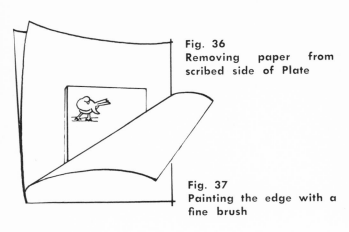

Fig. 36
Removing paper from scribed side of Plate

Fig. 37
Painting the edge with a fine brush

Step 9

Remove the paper that now covers the scribed side (see Fig. 36), wait six or seven minutes for the asphaltum underneath to set, and then clean the scribed surface, being careful not to eliminate the scribed lines. Cleaning the copper with steel wool helps the asphaltum to adhere firmly to the copper. Dirt enables the acid to creep under the asphaltum. Avoid fingerprints as you work by placing a piece of paper or a clean cloth under your hand on the clean copper, exposing only the parts you are about to paint. Paint with asphaltum the parts of the design that are to be protected from the acid. These will give the desired raised effect in the finished article.

Step 10

For a clean edge on your design, paint the edges first, with a fine brush. (See Figs. 37 and 38.) Then with the slightly larger brush fill in the mass. You will find it a great help in following the scribed lines to keep before you always your tracing of the design. (See Fig. 39.)

Always keep a small jar of turpentine handy, too, and a soft cloth, when you paint with asphaltum. Dip your brush into the turpentine frequently and dry it immediately with the cloth. This cleans out the thickened as-

Fig. 38
Close-up of above

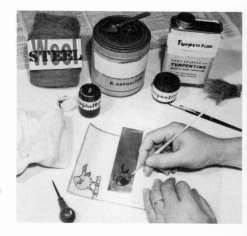

Fig. 39
Painting in the mass with heavier brush

Fig. 40
Correcting error in
asphaltum painting

phaltum and restores to your brush the flexibility that is important in asphaltum painting.

If you make a mistake in a spot where you have space to wash it out with turpentine, do so. Remove with steel wool the brown stain that is sometimes left, and repaint the part. If the mistake occurs in a spot where washing it out is not possible because of damage to the rest of the design, let it go for the time being. Continue painting the rest of your design until the asphaltum has dried somewhat. Then, with your scriber or the point of your brush handle, you can scrape off the excess at the point of error. Scrape gently back to the line of your design, and the mistake is rectified. (See Fig. 40.)

Step 11

After the design is completely painted, and all necessary surfaces are covered with asphaltum, check again for reddish spots. Check the outside of the edges, down to the paper; make sure that all are covered. Then paint with asphaltum beyond the edge, *onto the paper,* for about ¼ inch all around. (See Fig. 41.) Let the plate dry overnight and then trim the paper all around to about 2 inches beyond the edge of the plate.

Fig. 41
Painting asphaltum out on to paper to protect edges of copper

Step 12—Etching

Your plate is now ready to etch.

You must next decide which etching solution you will use—a mordant, or nitric acid.

Mordants are put out by craft supply houses for use in etching metals. They take the place of corrosive acids such as nitric, and are widely used in schools because of their safety factor. They will not harm the skin or clothing and are therefore preferable in some cases, especially in a kitchen workshop, with children about.

You can buy mordant for etching copper in solid or liquid form. The solid mordant comes in chunks which dissolve in water; the etch is slow, but sure and safe. It takes from twelve to twenty-four hours—sometimes longer—but it can be covered and left with complete safety, throughout the night if necessary.

The liquid mordant available on the market is used full-strength with no additional preparation. It takes an average of from two to five hours for a creditable etch on copper; this is about the same time as nitric acid, but the etch is not quite as sharp.

Nitric acid takes from one-and-a-half to five hours on copper, depending on the freshness and strength of the acid and on the prevailing temperature. This is the medium used by experienced craftsmen and professionals; and if you have a workshop, you will surely want to try it. With proper attention, it gives a clear clean etch; it does require care in handling, and you must decide if for you the good results justify the added care.

Basically, for all three solutions, we find that clean metal, plus well-painted asphaltum with cleanly outlined edges on the design, plus an etching solution done for the proper length of time, produces a good etching result.

Regardless of which solution you use, glass is required for the etching bin because neither acid nor mordant will eat into the glass or have any chemical effect upon it. Be assured that your glass or pyrex dish is completely safe for re-use in the kitchen after being used for etching. Merely rinse well with cold water, then wash with hot soap suds, then rinse and dry as in ordinary use.

Your glass or pyrex dish for this project should be about 8 inches square. If it is oblong or round, it should be large enough to let your 6-inch plate lie flat with a small space around it. The space is necessary to facilitate lifting the plate from the etching bath with the two clothespins. We suggest clothespins because of their availability. While they can be slid onto the edge of the plate to lift it, it is safer to raise the etched copper by slipping the clothespins underneath the project, with the copper resting on the flat side. Two flat pieces of wood (not pencils) would serve the same purpose. You will need to lift out the plate occasionally to examine the depth of the etch. (See Fig. 42.) Therefore, with the square plate you are etching

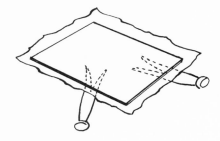

Fig. 42
One method of lifting project out of etching bath

the 8-inch square bin is good—a container that is too large wastes your solution.

In order to determine how much liquid you will need in your container, do this. Measure enough plain water into your container to reach a depth of about ½ inch, which is the depth your solution should be for an effective etch, regardless of which etching medium you are using. As you pour the water out, measure the amount you have used. You will find that an 8-inch square pyrex dish takes about two cups of liquid to reach the ½ inch level.

Because the depth of the solution is important in etching, an etch that is to be even in depth at all points requires that the bin be placed on as level a surface as possible during the etching. (See Fig. 43.)

ETCHING WITH SLOW MORDANT

(Step A)   If you are using the slow mordant, you will need to dissolve the chunks in water. (See Fig. 44.) Dissolve one pound of solid mordant chunks in one quart of water in a glass jar. (Step B) When the solution is ready, pour the necessary amount into the etching bin. (Step C) Slide in the copper plate (design side up) which has dried overnight, and mark down the time. (Step D) Because this will be a long-drawn-out etching time, cover your container and set it out of the way. Be sure it is set on a *level* surface. If you rock the container gently from time to time, to agitate the solution, you may shorten the etching time somewhat. (Step E) Examine the plate at long intervals to determine the progress of the etch. Take out the plate with the clothespins, *rinse it in water,* and inspect the etching carefully. (Step F) If you run your fingernail lightly over the part of the

Fig. 43
A *level* surface makes an even etch

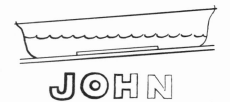

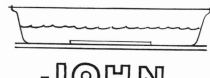

32

Fig. 44
Materials for etching copper with slow mordant

design not covered with asphaltum, and slide it gently to the edge of the asphaltum, you will feel a definite ridge that follows the outline of the design at the asphaltum edge. A deep etch removes about one third of the thickness of your copper; but not all designs call for so deep an etch, and you may not wish it. In estimating the depth of the etch, remember that the asphaltum itself adds a tiny part to the depth. A deep etch shows a thin line of bright copper under the edge of asphaltum along the design. When that is seen, always remove the piece from the etching bin at once. Wash it in clear cold water, dry it well, and proceed to clean it in turpentine as directed in Step 13.

ETCHING WITH THE FASTER (LIQUID) COPPER MORDANT

This is used as purchased (See Fig. 45.) Fill the etching bin with this solution up to the ½-inch depth, and then follow the same procedure as with the slow mordant, except for the timing. After you have put your project into the solution and marked down the time, begin to watch the progress of the etch after the first hour, at 20- to 30-minute intervals. This mordant is used full strength, just as it is purchased. When it begins to show signs of a definite etch, examine the plate carefully, lift with the clothespins, rinse in cold water, and test the ridge at the edge of your design gently with your fingernail as described. If not yet ready, return the copper to the etching bin. If ready, wash the plate in cold water, dry it, and follow the cleaning in turpentine procedure described in Step 13.

Fig. 45
Materials for etching copper with faster mordant

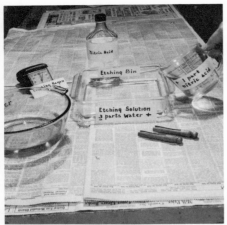

Fig. 46
Add *nitric acid* to water in etching bin

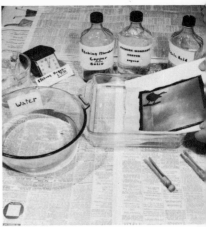

Fig. 47
Sliding the Plate into etching solution

ETCHING WITH NITRIC ACID

If you plan to use nitric acid, you can purchase it from your druggist. Because of its corrosive quality it is listed as a poison, and he will require you to sign his register for it, in accordance with a federal law. Although nitric acid is a liquid, it is sold by the pound, and one pound equals approximately one fluid pint.

It is well to say at this point that a healthy respect for acid is a valuable quality in a craftsman. If you wear glasses, be sure to wear them when working with acid. If a drop should splash on your skin, wash it off immediately in cold water and no harm will be done. You do not have to fear the acid if you follow carefully the simple procedures given here. By exercising *normal care,* the authors have *never had an accident* during twenty years of craft work with groups of all ages.

Before you begin to prepare the nitric acid etching solution, set the empty glass container on a level spot where it can remain undisturbed for the period of the etch. Nitric acid is not used in its full strength; we find the solution of 1 part of nitric to 3 parts of water works well on these etched projects. Therefore, in the 8-inch pyrex dish the 2 cups of liquid required will be made up of 1½ cups of water and ½ cup of nitric acid. The procedure in preparing the solution and handling the projects being etched is very exacting and must be followed carefully.

(*Step A*) Into the empty glass container pour 3 parts of clear cold water. *The water is always poured in first.* (See Fig. 46.) The concentrated acid has come to you from the druggist in a glass bottle with a glass stopper. Measure the 1 part of nitric acid in a glass measuring cup, re-cork the bottle at once, and set it away safely. Slowly, to avoid splashing, pour the acid from

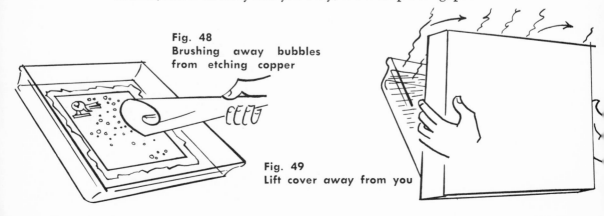

Fig. 48
Brushing away bubbles from etching copper

Fig. 49
Lift cover away from you

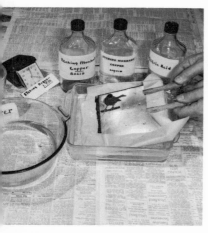

Fig. 50
Lifting Copper Plate out
of etching bin

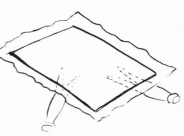

Fig. 51
Alternate method of lift-
ing Copper Plate out of
etching bin

the measuring cup into the water in the etching bin and rinse the cup in cold water immediately. Stand upright when measuring and pouring acid, as the fumes rise. Wash your hands at once.

Remember: The water is poured into the bin first; *the acid is always poured into the water.* This is very important!

(*Step B*) Stir the water and acid gently with a clothespin (on which there is no metal). (*Step C*) After a minute or two, gently slide the plate into the solution (design-side up), and mark down the time. (See Fig. 47.)

(*Step D*) In a few minutes bubbles will begin to form over the parts of the copper plate not covered by asphaltum. From time to time, brush these away gently with a roll of newsprint. (See Fig. 48.)

(*Step E*) Cover the bin with a piece of wood or cardboard or glass. Best of all, set over the bin a larger glass dish or a cardboard or wooden box, turned upside down, to enclose the bin completely. (See Fig. 49.) When you lift this large cover to examine your etch, always lift it so the fumes escape away from you. (See Fig. 49.) These fumes are not inflammable, so you need not worry about your pilot light or gas refrigerator, but they are irritating if you breathe them directly.

(*Step F*) Have ready at hand either running cold water or a glass bowl (or an enamel basin with no chipped places) full of cold water. After an hour or so, lift out the copper plate by the two clothespins. (See Fig. 50.) Remember, you do not need to clip the pins on the plate, but can slip them gently under the rim (see Fig. 51) and slip the plate into the basin of cold water or under the running water. (See Fig. 52.) (*Step G*) You can then hold the plate in your hand to examine the depth of etch already achieved. Run your fingernail against the edge of the design, and remember to allow for the thin layer of asphaltum in estimating the depth of etch. (See Fig. 53.)

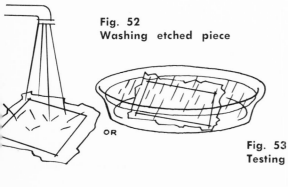

Fig. 52
Washing etched piece

OR

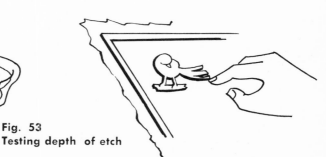

Fig. 53
Testing depth of etch

(*Step H*) Return the plate to the solution. (*Step I*) Cover it. (*Step J*) Always wash your hands. Change the rinsing water in the basin.

After the first hour, the etching process should be examined fairly often. There will be variations in etching time, depending on several factors. On a very hot day, or in a very warm room, the acid will work somewhat faster. Fresh acid will be more potent than re-used acid or acid that has been standing for some time. Even in freshly bought acid there is often variation in strength. An acid solution can be used on copper again and again, if it is bottled and capped immediately after use, but its strength is somewhat lessened each time, and a longer etching time will be needed for projects etched in such a solution. Each etching time must be watched under its own particular circumstances.

If your plate is etching properly, and all edges are well protected, let it continue until you consider it deep enough. If on examination the asphaltum on the edges is beginning to wash away, decide whether the etch is deep enough. If it is, remove the plate from the solution, wash it, and clean it. However, if you would like to etch it deeper, rinse the plate well in cold water, dry it thoroughly, and repaint the parts that need protection. Give the freshly painted asphaltum several hours to dry before replacing the plate in the acid bath.

A deep etch is more likely to appear with the nitric acid solution than with the mordants. The line of bright copper that appears under the asphaltum means a really deep etch, one that is certainly down one-third of the copper. It makes a handsome etch, but when this line appears, always remove the piece from the etching solution at once. (See Fig. 54 for review of etching steps.)

Fig. 54
REVIEW   OF   STEPS   IN   ETCHING

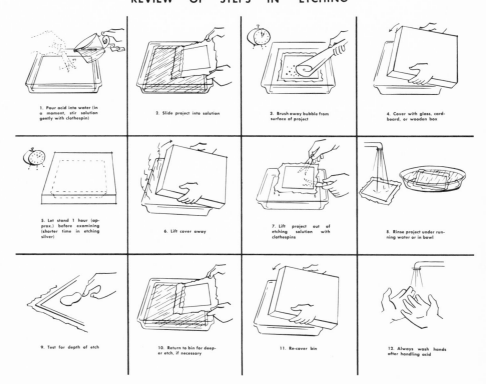

1. Pour acid into water (in a moment, stir solution gently with clothespin)

2. Slide project into solution

3. Brush away bubble from surface of project

4. Cover with glass, cardboard, or wooden box

5. Let stand 1 hour (approx.) before examining (shorter time in etching silver)

6. Lift cover away

7. Lift project out of etching solution with clothespins

8. Rinse project under running water or in bowl

9. Test for depth of etch

10. Return to bin for deeper etch, if necessary

11. Re-cover bin

12. Always wash hands after handling acid

Fig. 55
Soak off asphaltum in turpentine

Fig. 56
Rub with steel wool to hasten cleaning

Step 13—Cleaning off the Asphaltum

When the etch is deep enough, take out the plate, rinse it very well in cold water, and dry it. Place it in a glass bowl, pie plate, or enamel basin. Pour turpentine over it to cover, and allow it to stand until the asphaltum and paper come off easily. (See Fig. 55.) Rubbing with steel wool will help to hasten the cleaning up. (See Fig. 56.) Wear rubber gloves to protect your hands from stains from the asphaltum and the turpentine in this operation.

Step 14

(A)   Pour the nitric acid solution into a glass bottle with a wide mouth and a glass stopper and put it away safely. It can be used again for copper etching.

(B)   When the asphaltum is washed off your plate by the turpentine, and dried with a soft cloth, you will find the first sight of your raised design very thrilling indeed. (See Fig. 57.) The excitement of this first view will be repeated with every project coming out of the acid, no matter how many objects you make. It is part of the satisfaction in creating fine things.

Dry your plate thoroughly and clean it well with steel wool. Bottle and save the used turpentine. It can be used again and again.

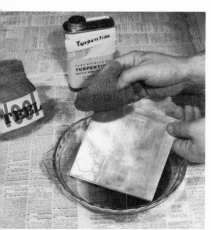

Fig. 57
Etched Plate with asphaltum and paper removed

Step 15—Shaping the Plate

You are now ready to shape your plate. You will need the following materials:

1 round-nosed wooden mallet
1 buckskin mallet
1 mold with 3-inch hollow (indentation)
1 piece of liver of sulphur (purchased from druggist)
1 compass
  Scotch Tape

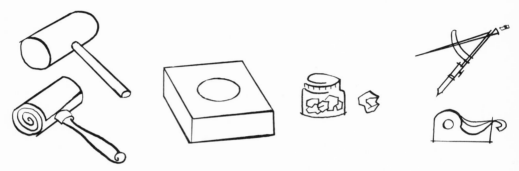

Before shaping your plate, it is necessary to hammer the square of copper absolutely flat. The buckskin mallet—sometimes called a rawhide mallet—is used so that hammer marks will not appear on the plate. However, a little practice with this tool is suggested; practice hitting the mallet on a piece of soft wood until you can consistently strike it flat without leaving edge marks. (See Fig. 58.) This technique is required in all shaping of metals, and it is not difficult to master. When you are ready, place your plate on the floor and flatten it with your buckskin mallet. Do not hammer longer than is necessary; beating copper hardens it.

**Fig. 58
Right and wrong way to
flatten metal with buckskin
mallet**

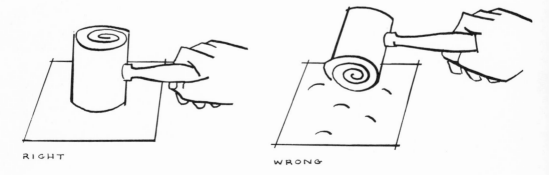

RIGHT   WRONG

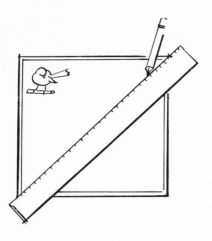

Fig. 59
**Ruling penciled line to find
center of Plate**

Fig. 60
**Making circle as guide for
shaping**

Step 16

Now lay your copper square on the table, etched side up. Rule a penciled line diagonally across the plate from corner to corner (see Fig. 59); rule one from the opposite corners. The point at which they meet is the exact center. Use your compass from this point to get a penciled circle 3 inches in diameter. (See Fig. 60.)

Step 17

Turn your plate over, face-down on the table. Lay the wooden mold upside down on the copper, evenly spaced on all sides. Lightly Scotch Tape it to the copper; it will hold for awhile until you locate the hollow with your mallet. (See Fig. 61.)

Fig. 61
Fastening copper to mold

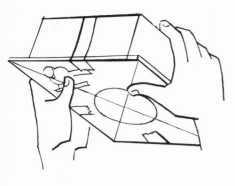

Fig. 62
Turning copper and mold right side up

Fig. 63
First marks to establish the hollow

Step 18

Turn copper and mold right side up. (See Fig 62.) Hold the copper firmly on the mold and tap smartly with the round-nosed wooden mallet—¼ inch within the penciled circle. Start at south, then one tap at north, then west, then east. (See Fig. 63.) This marks the placement of the hollow. Then, still holding the copper firmly on the mold, tap along the rim, always inside the circle. (See Fig. 64.) This outlines the hollow on the copper. Overlap your strokes so as to achieve a smooth outline, but do not attempt to hammer much below the rim into the depth of the hollow; you will find the slight indentation sufficient. Remove the plate from the mold and set it upside down on a flat surface. Flatten all parts of your plate outside the hollow with your buckskin mallet. (See Fig. 65.)

Now turn your plate right side up and check to see whether it sits flat. If it doesn't, check for sections of your rim that have been tapped too lightly. Mark these spots in pencil on the right side of the plate. Return it to the mold and hammer lightly again on the marked sections. This should correct the uneven "stance." Polish your plate as brightly as possible with steel wool before the next step.

Step 19—Oxidizing

Your plate is now ready for oxidizing. Oxidizing (or antiquing) is the method employed to darken the background of a design and to heighten the effect by highlighting its bright surfaces.

Place a piece of liver of sulphur the size of a green pea in a small dish and pour very hot water over it to dissolve it. Its smell is offensive (like bad eggs), but this operation takes just a moment, and the liquid can then be thrown out. Dip a brush or a rag into the mixture and wipe it quickly over

Fig. 64
Completing the hollow

Fig. 65
Flattening the rim of the shaped Plate

Fig. 66
Beginning to oxidize Plate

the entire surface of the finished plate. (See Figs. 66 and 67.) It will darken immediately, but do not feel that your high shine is lost; it will be restored by re-polishing. Allow the plate to dry while you throw out the evil-smelling liquid. Try not to get any on your hands; it leaves a yellow stain that takes time to wear off.

Step 20

Now polish your plate again lightly with steel wool. You will find that the design has held the darkness in the recesses. Do not attempt to polish that away. Merely highlight the surface of your etched design by polishing away *some* of the oxidizing. Rub the rest of your plate to the high polish you had before. You will find that the oxidizing has given even the re-polished parts a modified gleam that is very good-looking.

Handsome copper pieces demand little care to remain so. There are several copper cleaners on the market that will help you keep copper objects clean without too much effort. After awhile, the copper achieves a patina (finish) that is beautiful in itself. However, some craftsmen prefer to lacquer their pieces to avoid re-polishing. If you wish to do so, there are good sprays on the market that come with explicit directions for their use. Follow their instructions for good results.

A set of four of these plates makes a handsome gift. Used at home for snacks at tea or bridge, such a set always causes pleasant comment. You can make a set with a different bird pose on each plate, another with a different initial for each member of the family. There is, of course, no limit to variations. The modern letter is shown also, as the plate itself is modern in feeling, and some prefer the simplicity of the block initial.

Fig. 67
Plate completely oxidized

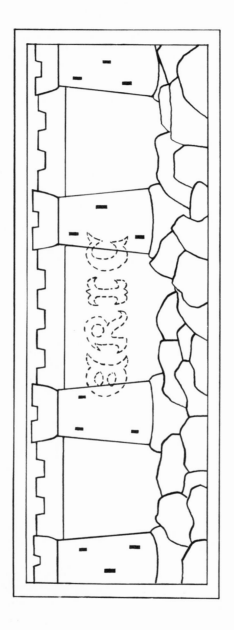

Fig. 68
Exact size for tracing

42

Chapter 3

BOY'S NAPKIN RING—Later a Desk Blotter and Paper Weight

IN ADDITION TO THE MATERIALS ON HAND, YOU WILL NEED, TO BEGIN:

1 piece of 18-gauge copper 6½ x 2¼ inches
   straight tinsnips
1 piece of ⅜-inch dowel, 6 inches
   small vise—for desk blotter and paper weight

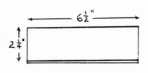
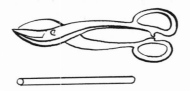
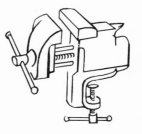

This is designed primarily as a gift for a baby boy, but it can be used for any child, boy or girl. It is inexpensive, and this design is particularly suited to the type of name used, though other names can be used with it. Keep an open mind and be receptive to any combination of names and designs that appeals to you. Instructions here follow this design specifically, as it is reproduced in Fig. 68, drawn to size.

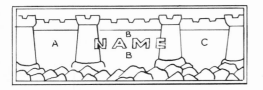

Fig. 69
Spaces A, B, and C, on
which to scribe "bricks"

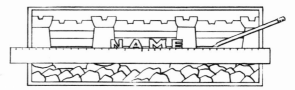

Fig. 70
Drawing horizontal lines

Step 1

While this project uses the same techniques as in previous plans, it goes
one step further and starts one step earlier. Cut out your copper to the
required size with the tinsnips, then follow all steps as in earlier projects
(bevel, design, trace, scribe, paint asphaltum, etch—see Chapter 2 for
techniques) until you come to taking the copper out of the acid. Rinse it in
cold water and clean it as usual with turpentine and steel wool.

Step 2

For the next step (indicating bricks on the design) you will need your
sharp scriber and your ruler. Mark out in pencil on the copper, on A, B, and
C (see Fig. 69), lines approximately ³⁄₁₆ of an inch apart. (See Fig. 70.)
Then draw alternate connecting lines to represent bricks. (See Fig. 71.)
The pencil marks can be drawn with a ruler. Follow these lines with your
scriber, pressing quite hard for a deep clear line. Try if possible to follow the
penciled lines with the scriber *without* a ruler, so as to avoid a machine-made
look. Then clean off the pencil marks with steel wool. Rubbing the scribed
lines lightly with steel wool softens their outlines on the copper. Clean the
strip back and front. It is now ready to bend into a napkin ring form.

Fig. 71
Drawing connecting lines
to make "bricks"

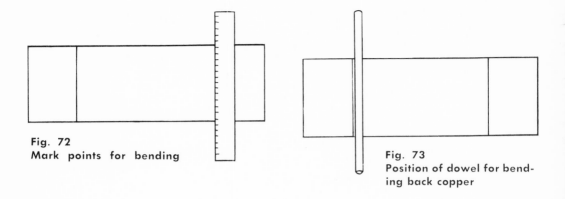

Fig. 72
Mark points for bending

Fig. 73
Position of dowel for bending back copper

Step 3

Turn your copper strip face-down, draw a pencil line across each short end 1 $\frac{13}{16}$ inches from the end. (See Fig. 72.) Lay your piece of dowel across the copper along the inner edge of the line. (See Fig. 73.) Holding the dowel firmly in place, press the copper strip upward over it. (See Fig. 74.) Complete the turn by tapping lightly with the buckskin mallet. If you prefer, place the dowel firmly in your vise. Hold the copper strip against the dowel in the same position as in Fig. 73. Lightly tap the end over the dowel with the buckskin mallet. (See Fig. 75.) Do the same for the other end, and your napkin ring is shaped.

Polish and oxidize with fresh liver of sulphur and polish again to bring out the highlights (as described in Chapter 2).

Fig. 74
Folding copper on table by hand method

Fig. 75
Folding Napkin Ring with dowel in vise

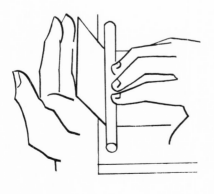

DESK BLOTTER AND PAPERWEIGHT

When your boy is old enough to get his first desk, mark the occasion by changing his napkin ring to a desk blotter and paper weight.

In the case of the design shown, the change from napkin ring to desk blotter came when the boy's reading was full of knights in armour and stories of medieval days. The familiar design received fresh notice and appreciation in its new form. The perennial interests of small boys and big can be utilized for design ideas. Silhouettes or line drawings of trains, planes, or even maps would be suitable and good-looking in the later form as well as being acceptable in the earlier form. Whatever design you choose, think of one that will please the small boy and still be acceptable to him in later years.

You will need for this blotter:

1 piece of hardwood 5 x 2¼ x 1⅛ inches (maple or birch will do)
1 brush for shellac
  shellac
  stain (optional)
  blotter 9½ x 2¼ inches
1 crosscut saw
1 combination square
1 sheet sandpaper 1/0

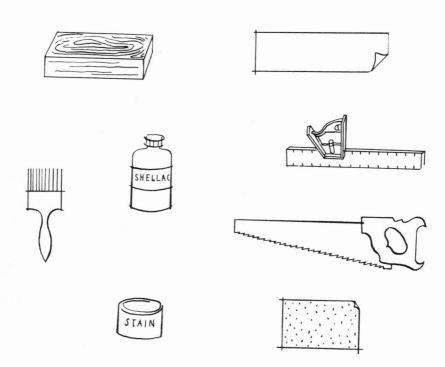

Fig. 76
Straightening Napkin Ring
by hand

Fig. 77
Flattening with buckskin
mallet

Step 1

Straighten the folds of the napkin ring by hand. (See Fig. 76.) Tap lightly with the mallet on a hardwood surface to flatten all bends, turning the metal over and hammering on both sides, if necessary. (See Fig. 77.)

Step 2

Now you are ready to prepare the wood for your desk blotter.

Ask your lumber dealer to cut your wood to size if possible. Many lumber yards supply such a service. If they do not, cut your board to $\frac{1}{16}$ of an inch larger than the dimensions given above and sand it down to size. Be careful not to round off the edges. A small flat block of any wood around which you can wrap a small piece of sandpaper will help keep your sharp edges. (See Fig. 78.)

Fig. 78
Method of sanding to keep
edges sharp

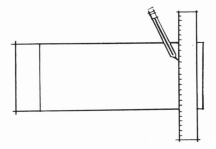

Fig. 79
Marking copper for bending

Step 3

When your wood is cut, decide whether you prefer a light finish for con-trast with the copper or a dark stain to match a mahogany or walnut desk. If you prefer a light finish, buy *four- or five-pound cut shellac* (available at hardware stores) in small amounts. Apply a thin coat to one side of your wood and allow it to dry for at least a half hour (until the wood is no longer sticky). Then paint another surface and allow that to dry. Repeat for all sur-faces and edges. Sand lightly with the sandpaper and apply another coat of shellac to each surface.

If you prefer a dark finish on your wood, wipe on your chosen color of stain with a soft cloth. Let it absorb a few minutes and then rub it off across the grain. If it is still too light, apply the stain again and allow it to stand longer, and again rub it off across the grain. Allow it to dry 24 hours. Then follow directions for shellac.

Fig. 80
Protecting copper before bending

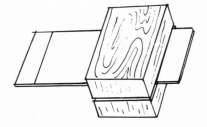

Fig. 81
Tapping ends over wood
block in vise

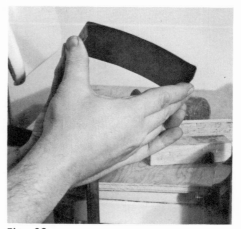

Fig. 82
Adjusting ends to grip
wooden base for Blotter

Step 4

On the back of your copper strip, measure in ¾ of an inch from one end and draw a pencil line parallel to the short edge. (See Fig. 79.) Repeat at the other end. Place the copper between two pieces of wood to protect it (see Fig. 80) and set it into the vise. Allow one end of the copper to project just enough to show the line you have drawn above the wood strips which hold it. With the buckskin mallet tap the copper on the etched side so that it folds over at a 90° angle. Reverse it in the vise and repeat at opposite end. (See Fig. 81.) By hand, press in the copper ends just a bit so that they will grip somewhat the ends of your wood block. (See Fig. 82.)

Step 5

Cut your blotter exactly 9½ x 2¼ inches. Give your copper a last polish and set the blotter around the bottom edge of the wood so that it fits up over the ends. (See Fig. 83.) Place the copper over it and clip into place.

Fig. 83
Slipping tight copper over
blotter-covered wooden base

sing of simple things · that all men share · are

Chapter 4

A GIFT PLATE OR "NAME PLATE" IN COPPER

In addition to the materials on hand, you will need, to begin:

1 disk of 18-gauge copper 8 inches in diameter
1 mold with a 4-inch hollow
   rubber cement

 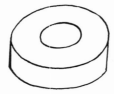

This plate was originally used as a child's "name-plate." The inspiration for it was a pleasant old-fashioned custom of presenting the new baby in a family with a plate on which his name was engraved or painted. That custom has been followed in a family where now four children, and the parents, too, have each acquired a plate. This interesting row of name-bearing plates on a shelf or Welsh cabinet makes an attractive display.

In our project, a variation is shown, in that we used a line of poetry instead of a name. If extreme simplicity is desired, the two bands are sufficient decoration. (See Fig. 84.) They must be painted carefully for a smooth clear edge. However, the raised letters add much to the effect. It is possible with this to make a gift of great personal value without any great expenditure.

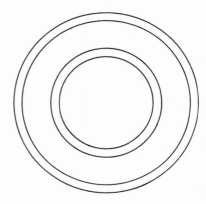

Fig. 84
Two bands for a simple design

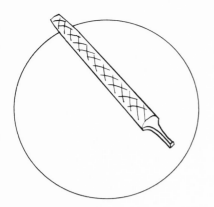

Fig. 85
Bevel the copper edge as usual

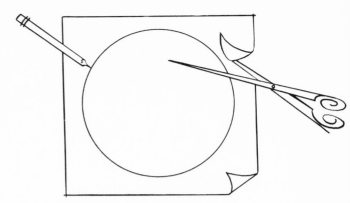

Fig. 86
Cutting tracing paper to size of copper Plate

All processes used in making this plate follow those used in making the tea plate, and all materials and tools used for Chapter 2 are now on hand for this project. With one addition. The mold to be used for shaping this plate requires a hollow with a 4-inch diameter.

You are now ready to prepare your design. The following steps may sound complicated, but they are actually simple to do.

Step 1

To personalize your design and make it suit your individual needs, the name or the wording used is important. Therefore, the style of lettering chosen should be suited to the person or to the character of the saying.

We begin as usual with a sheet of tracing paper cut to the size of our project. As in the tea plate procedure, the edge of our 8-inch circle of copper is first beveled (see Fig. 85) and then outlined with pencil on a sheet of tracing paper. (See Figs. 85 and 86.)

Fig. 87

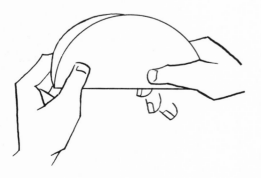

Fig. 88
Finding the center of a circle

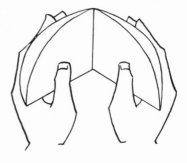

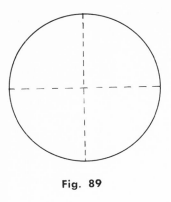

Fig. 89

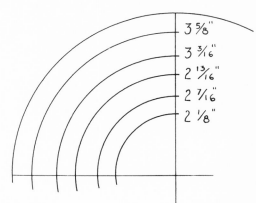

3 ⅝"
3 3/16"
2 13/16"
2 7/16"
2 ⅛"

Fig. 90
Exact measurement for circular bands

Step 2

Cut out this circle. (See Fig. 86.) Fold this sheet once, carefully matching the edges. (See Fig. 87.) Then crease the fold with your thumb. Fold again in the opposite direction so that the crease is at right angles. (See Fig. 88.) Where the creases cross is the exact center. (See Fig. 89.)

Step 3

Use this point to center your compass. Now draw five penciled circles, one at each of these distances from the center: 2⅛ inches, 2⁷⁄₁₆ inches, 2¹³⁄₁₆ inches, 3³⁄₁₆ inches, 3⅝ inches. (See Figs. 90 and 91.)

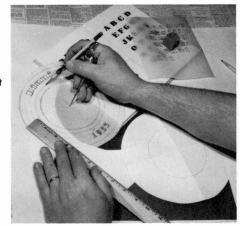

Fig. 91
Preparing design sheet

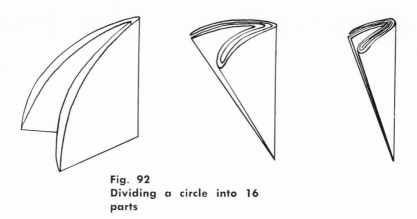

Fig. 92
Dividing a circle into 16
parts

Step 4

To prepare your lettering in this design, you will need directional lines for guidance in placing your letters. Refold your sheet in the same creases to form the quarter-circle. Starting firmly from the center, fold again and mark the crease with your thumb. Repeat once again and crease firmly. (See Fig. 92.) Open your circle, and rule penciled lines along each crease across the circle. You now have sixteen divisions. (See Fig. 93.) Rule a line to divide each division in half. (See Fig. 94.) You now have a circle divided into thirty-two parts, by radiating lines. These lines indicate the position your letters will take around the circle.

A good letter design manual, showing several styles of alphabets, is an important aid to lettering. However, it is well to develop the habit of watching for interesting kinds of type in newspapers and magazines. Artists cut out and save examples of interesting material they may use at some future time. Once your interest is aroused, you will find many examples of words and types of letters you will want to cut out and put away. A large manila envelope or a folder kept handy for these idea-sparkers will be a source of great help to you from time to time. You will find yourself doing this also for all kinds of design. It is a very rewarding procedure.

The letters on this plate were chosen from *Modern Alphabet,* by Melbert B. Cary, Jr., published by Bridgman Publishers, page 48.

Fig. 93
Lines drawn on creases to
make 16 divisions

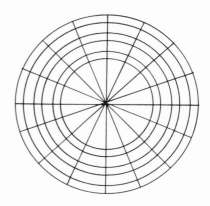

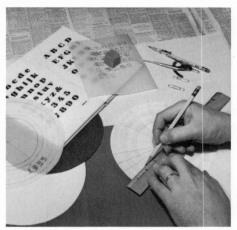

Fig. 94
Dividing each segment to
make 32 divisions

Fig. 95
Traced letters are cut out
for easy placement

Step 5

Decide on the words that are to go on your plate and the style of type you will use. Trace copies of all the letters you will need, and cut them out. (See Fig. 95.)

On your prepared 8″ circle of tracing paper, mark the two circles that form the top and bottom boundaries of the letters. (See Fig. 96, *shaded area.*) On this band formed by the two circles lay out your words with the cut-out letters you have prepared.

Your first layout will necessarily be experimental, partly because of the different width of the letters. However, you can determine which letter you will place in the middle of the band at the top, then work to right and left. The wheeling lines you have drawn on your design sheet will help you to establish the vertical position of each letter. (See Fig. 97.) When you have arranged the letters to your liking, cement each in place with rubber cement. You are now ready to make your clean copy to use in transferring the design to the metal.

Fig. 96
Shaded band indicates lo-
cation of letters

Fig. 97
Wheeling lines help to
keep letters vertical

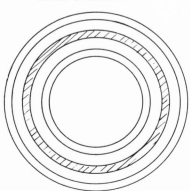

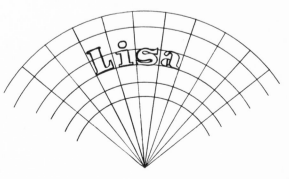

Fig. 98
Tracing fresh design sheet

Step 6

Prepare another 8″ circle of tracing paper. Set in your circular lines by compass as before. Line up your tracing paper exactly edge to edge over the first trial sheet, and make a clean copy of the letters in position between the bordering lines you have already drawn. (See Fig. 98.) This is your clean copy.

Step 7

Follow directions for transferring the design to copper, as in Chapter 2. (See Fig. 99.) When the design is transferred to the white-painted copper to your satisfaction, scribe exactly as described in Chapter 2. However, to scribe in the circular lines A, D, and E in Fig. 100, use a compass that has a sharp metal point in place of the pencil. This is called a pair of dividers. It will be more accurate than following the penciled circle with a scriber. Remember, *trace*, but *do not scribe* circles B and C which form the band on which the letters are placed. (See Fig. 100.) Though you do not *scribe* these lines, leave the penciled circles on the plate to help you when you scribe the letters.

Fig. 99
Fresh design sheet ready to trace onto white-painted copper

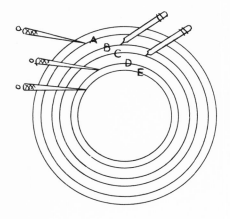

Fig. 100
Three circles to be scribed
and two left penciled

Step 8

Clean your plate well with steel wool, and paint the back with asphaltum as in Chapter 2. Turn the plate over on the newsprint. Clean the front ready for painting and lay the clean piece of paper under your hand.

If painting in the letters seems most challenging to you, start with those. Then do the bands between the lines D and E, and A to the edge of the plate. (See Figs. 100 and 101.) Do not forget when the painting is done, to extend the asphaltum beyond the copper edge and on to the paper for ¼ of an inch. (See Fig. 101.) Let it dry overnight.

Fig. 101
Painting the border and
beyond

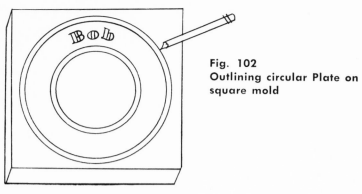

Fig. 102
Outlining circular Plate on
square mold

Step 9

Etch as before in copper mordant or nitric acid, following directions in
Chapter 2. Clean in turpentine and polish with steel wool.

Step 10

Now you are ready to shape your plate.

If your mold with the 4-inch hollow is square, lay your copper plate
exactly in the middle of it, keeping all margins equal, and draw a penciled
line on the mold around the copper. This is to help you keep the plate in
place on the mold while shaping it. (See Fig. 102.)

Your problem is simpler if the 4-inch hollow is set in a circular 8-inch
mold. You have then only to make sure that you keep all edges lined up
while you hammer your plate. (See Fig. 103.) Follow all directions for
shaping as given for the tea plate in Chapter 2.

You will find that the hollow in this plate comes just within the inner circle
of the design. Therefore all your design will be on the flat part of your plate.
This is a part of the decorative quality of this plate—on wall or shelf, or on
an easily constructed wire stand.

Step 11

Polish, oxidize, and polish again as in Chapter 2.

Your personal needs can lead to wide variations; first and second name or
full, separate initials, or a line of poetry shared with the potential receiver of
the gift. There are many occasions to make this a single gift plate, or in
family sets up to any number. Possible variations are endless.

Fig. 103
Shaping circular Plate on
circular mold

Chapter 5

LITTLE GIRL'S SILVER NAPKIN RING—Later a Bracelet

IN THIS PROJECT DO *not* BEVEL THE EDGE OF THE METAL. INSTEAD, OUTLINE the silver strip with pencil on a piece of tracing paper. Within that frame work out the design on the paper.

In addition to the materials on hand, you will need, to begin:

1 strip of 20-gauge sterling silver 1 x 5⅛
    inches
1 jeweler's saw and blades #1 or #2
1 small piece of ¼-inch plywood 2½ x 6
    inches
1 piece of ⅜-inch dowel 5 or 6 inches long
1 crosscut saw or coping saw
1 small C clamp
1 jeweler's half round file ⎫
1 jeweler's triangular file ⎭ These are needle files that can be bought singly or in sets

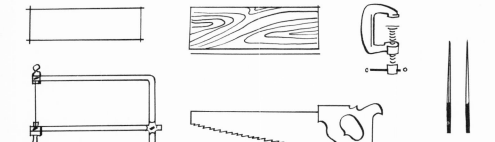

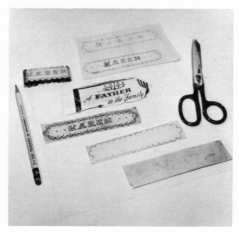

Fig. 104
Lettering style adapted
from newspaper clipping

Step 1

Proceed as before to make your design, incorporating any name you are planning to use. Beveling the edges comes later, after the scallops are cut.

Because the design shown was obviously taken from a dainty piece of embroidery of the nineties, a suitable style of type was used. This was taken from a newspaper advertisement of an old-fashioned play. (See Fig. 104.) The letter *K* was fashioned from the *R* with a slight change. The pattern can be traced exactly, as it is given full-size on this page. (See Fig. 105.) Prepare two clean copies of your tracing and outline the design on one in pen and ink. On the other, outline the scalloped edge with pen and ink, very carefully. Rubber cement this strip of paper onto your silver strip. Always place the design sheet as near the edge of the silver as possible. It saves both silver and labor in cutting with the jeweler's saw. Be sure you can see clearly the line you must follow with the jeweler's saw as you cut through the paper and silver. After cutting, the paper will be torn off and the silver cleaned of the rubber cement by rubbing with the fingers.

Fig. 105
Bracelet design drawn to size

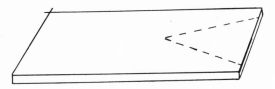

Fig. 106
Making a V board

Step 2

On the board clamped to your kitchen step-stool you must now clamp a smaller gadget—a V board to help in cutting the scalloped edge of the napkin ring. Cut out a V in the center of one end of the strip of wood to a depth of 2 inches. (See Fig. 106.)

Then fasten it to the working board with a C clamp with the V extending. (See Fig. 107.) The silver is to be held across this V while cutting the scallops with the jeweler's saw.

Fig. 107
Attaching V board to workbench

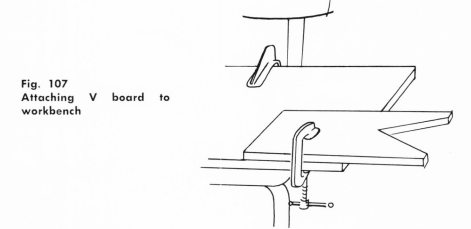

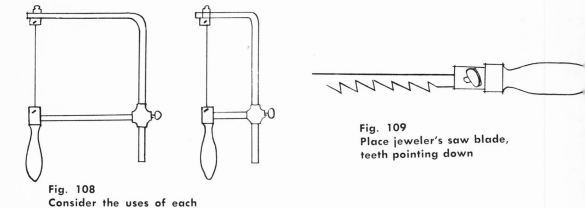

Fig. 108
Consider the uses of each
size of jeweler's saw

Fig. 109
Place jeweler's saw blade,
teeth pointing down

Step 3

For this napkin ring a small jeweler's saw with only a 3-inch span between blade and back will suffice. However, later projects will require a 6-inch or 8-inch span. So perhaps the large saw would be a wiser purchase at this time. (See Fig. 108.)

The blade in a jeweler's saw must be held taut between the screws. To achieve this taut blade, fasten it *teeth pointing down* in the handle end of the saw. (See Fig. 109.) Then press the upper part of the saw against a firm surface, and while pressing, slip the upper end of the blade in place and tighten the screw. (See Fig. 110.)

Fig. 110
Pressing head of saw
against hard surface to
insert taut blade

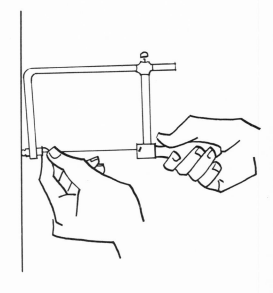

Fig. 111
Cutting silver across the V
board

Step 4

For effective cutting, the saw must be held absolutely vertical to your project, with the silver itself held firmly on the V board by thumb and fore-finger. The V board should be somewhat below eye level, in order to see clearly and keep the saw in proper position. If necessary, take a seat low enough to enable you to work at the proper eye level.

To cut your silver bracelet, hold it across the V board, and set your saw at a point of the scribed scallop that is nearest the edge of the silver. (See Fig. 111.) Follow the line of the design without pressing the blade forward. Sometimes a wax candle rubbed lightly on the saw smoothes the cutting. A little practice will be necessary—one or two of the blades will be broken at first, but the knack in using the saw comes quickly. Follow the scallop as it has been outlined on the pattern, turning the silver to feed to the saw along the line to be cut. (See Figs. 112 and 113.) When you come to the sharp angle between the scallops, continue to work the saw gently up and down, but pivot the silver at that point until the saw blade is in position to continue with the next scallop. Keep the smooth back edge of the saw blade against your cut portion as you turn the silver in the angle. Remember to

Fig. 112
Position of silver when cutting toward end of scallop

Fig. 113
Silver (not saw) turned around for cutting next scallop

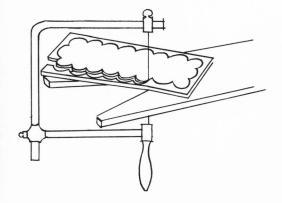

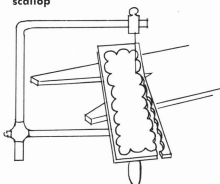

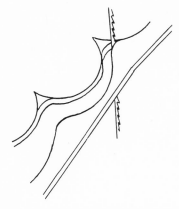

Fig. 114
Do not cut deeply between
scallops

keep your saw blade absolutely vertical at right angles to your silver. Do not cut *deeply* into the angle between the scallops. (See Fig. 114.) Allow yourself a slight margin to file down with the half round or triangular needle file. These small fine needle files are especially designed to work jewelry. They are necessary on small surfaces with a metal as soft as silver. In this case the flat side of either file can be used for the curve of the scallop (see Fig. 115) and the angled edge can be used to file between the scallops. (See Fig. 116.)

Many blades are broken in removing the saw from the work. If you must withdraw it, remember to keep up the sawing motion while you back the saw gently out of the cut you have made in the silver.

Step 5

When your scallops are all cut, bevel the edges smooth with the half round or triangular needle file, alternating with steel wool. Keep filing gently up and over, but remember that sterling silver is very soft, and do not exert as much pressure with your file as in beveling copper. Clean the right side with steel wool, and paint the silver strip with white tempera. When it dries, lay a strip of carbon paper and your design sheet on the scalloped silver strip, and trace and scribe in the rest of your design. This is the name and inside border of the scallops and the dots. (See Fig. 105.)

Fig. 115
Flat side of needle file for
beveling curves

Fig. 116
Angled edge of needle
file for beveling between
scallops

Step 6

You are now ready to paint your napkin ring with asphaltum. Clean and paint the back and turn it over on the newsprint. Clean and paint the front, and be very careful to protect the scalloped edges, deep into the angles, with the asphaltum. Paint the letters and the scallops very clearly, with clean smooth edges, as a delicate design such as this depends especially on crisp lines in the etch. Extend the painting, as in Chapter 2, beyond the edges, onto the paper for at least ¼ inch all around. Let your napkin ring dry overnight.

Step 7

You are now ready to etch your napkin ring.
You will need:

silver mordant or
clean nitric acid

A quite small glass dish will be sufficient for this project. Measure its capacity in water and decide whether you will etch your napkin ring in *silver* mordant, which takes 10 or 12 hours, or nitric acid (3 parts water to 1 of acid), which takes 1 to 2 hours and care in handling. (See Chapter 2.)

If you are using the *silver* mordant, pour the solution as it comes in the bottle into your etching dish to a depth of ½ inch. (See Fig. 117.) Slide in your napkin ring and prepare to leave it for 10 or 12 hours. It is a good idea to set the dish out of the way for this long period. Examine it every hour or so and rock the container gently at long intervals. This will hasten the etch somewhat. Always rinse the napkin ring in cold water when you take it out to examine the progress of the etch. See section on etching in Chapter 2, page 31.

Fig. 117
Etching silver with silver mordant

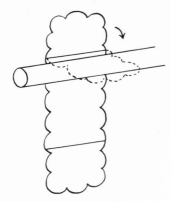

Fig. 118
Placing of silver against
dowel for shaping Napkin
Ring

If you are using nitric acid, follow the directions in Chapter 2, pages 34 to 36. Silver takes from 1 to 2 hours for a good etch (using a 3 to 1 solution), depending on the strength of the acid, its freshness, the temperature of the room, and general temperature. It must be examined after the first 30 minutes and every 20 minutes or so thereafter. Remember to follow instructions about the cold water rinse.

Use clean acid for silver. Acid that has been used for copper cannot be used for silver, nor can silver and copper pieces be etched together. Clean acid that has been used for etching silver can be used again for etching silver or copper, with due allowance for extra time for etching because of weakened acid. Silver is soft, and an etch that is left undisturbed often produces a delicately stippled effect on the background that is very effective.

Step 8

When your etch is completed, clean as in Chapter 2, page 37 and oxidize as on page 40. With fine steel wool rub over the highlights, leaving enough of the oxidizing in the background to bring out character in the design.

Fig. 119
Shaping silver Napkin Ring
by hand over dowel in vise

Fig. 120
Reshaping to Bracelet form

Step 9

You are now ready to shape your silver into the napkin ring form.

Measure 1¾₁₆ inches in from each end and with a pencil draw a line across the silver strip, as in the copper napkin ring in Chapter 4. Using the same method, place the ⅜-inch dowel in the vise, lay the strip against the dowel with the line showing (See Fig. 118.) and bend the napkin ring to shape by hand. (See Fig. 119.) Tap the ends in place with the buckskin mallet. Give a final quick buffing to polish highly.

BRACELET

When the little girl is old enough to wear a silver bracelet, straighten the ends of the napkin ring gently by hand and flatten the silver with a buckskin mallet. Because of the scallops, this bracelet tends to crease if simply bent to shape by hand. In order to round it to bracelet form, first lay the silver strip face down on a piece of hardwood. Then, holding one edge in the left hand (see Fig. 120), tap the length of the strip lightly with the buckskin mallet, slowly raising the strip with the left hand till the bracelet curves gently but evenly from the wood. *Then* shape the silver by hand into bracelet form by pressing it around the head of the wooden mallet, hammering lightly with the buckskin mallet to set the ends in line. (See Fig. 121.) Polish as usual with fine steel wool.

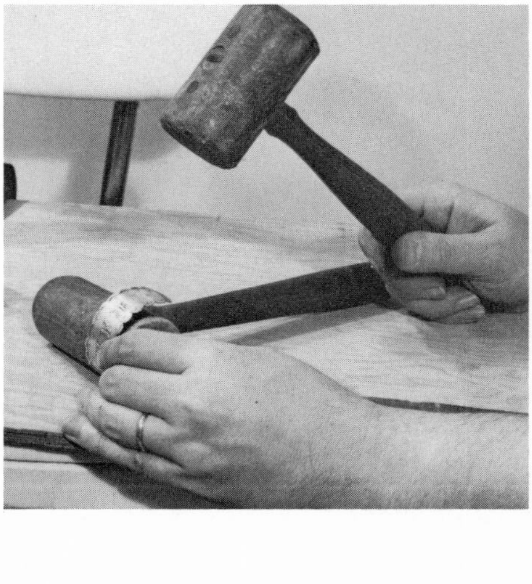

Fig. 121
Final shaping to Bracelet form

Chapter 6

CHILD'S STERLING SILVER NAME PLATE

In addition to materials at hand, you will need, to begin:

1 5-inch square of sterling silver, 20-gauge.

This is a variation of the 8-inch copper plate in Chapter 4 but is a more formal gift, because of its material. It employs the etching and jeweler's saw cutting techniques that have been used in previous projects, but is shown here as a suggestion either for a child's gift plate or for a set of bread and butter plates. In somewhat larger sizes, 6 or 7 inches, it is suitable for an individual salad or tea plate.

Step 1

In preparing this design, outline with pencil your 5-inch square of silver on your tracing paper, and cut *4* identical squares of tracing paper, each 5 x 5 inches. Lay 3 of them aside for the moment.

On one 5-inch square of tracing paper, rule diagonal lines connecting opposite corners across the plate. Where they cross is the center. Set your compass point at this center mark, and draw a 5-inch circle on your tracing paper. (See Fig. 122.) (In this project, as in making the silver napkin ring in Chapter 5, you do *not* begin by beveling the edges of the metal, as they will be cut away to the scalloped edge of the plate.)

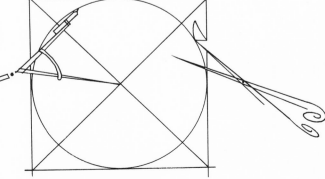

Fig. 122
First steps in preparing design sheet

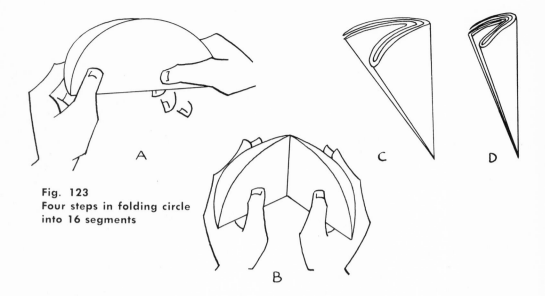

Fig. 123
Four steps in folding circle into 16 segments

A

B

C

D

Step 2

Cut out the paper circle. Fold it in half, lining up the edges carefully, and crease the fold sharply. Fold this in half again, and crease. Repeat this, always folding from the center until you have 8 segments. (See Fig. 123.) Then fold and crease once again, to give a guiding line to the divisions of the border, which you will use later. Trace the diagram of the segment (see Fig. 124) on this page and use it to mark the curve on the segment of your still folded design sheet and cut it away. (See Fig. 125.)

The design should then appear as in Fig. 126. Follow the patterned curve with an inner line $\frac{1}{16}$ inch away. This marks the border. (See Fig. 127.)

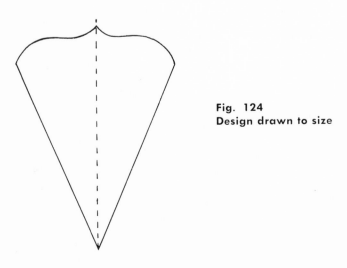

Fig. 124
Design drawn to size

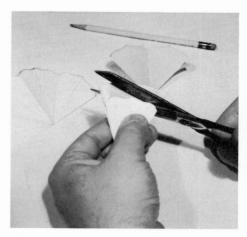

Fig. 125
Shaping the folded circle

Step 3

If the plate is to be personalized, trace out letters on another piece of tracing paper, until you have exactly the arrangement and size you like. Then paste this arrangement of letters on the design sheet of the plate, using either rubber cement or cellulose tape. This name (*jane*) is centered exactly above and below the middle line of the circle, equi-distant from each end.

(The lettering on this plate is from *Modern Alphabet*, by Melbert E. Carey, Jr., Bridgman Publishers, page 70.) The delicacy of the letters is in keeping with the grace of the border.

Fig. 126
Edge pattern of unfolded circle

Fig. 127
Marking the inner line of the border

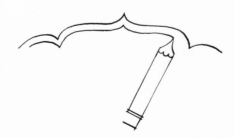

Step 4

Take the second of the 5-inch squares of tracing paper that were cut earlier. On this square lay the cut-out design sheet, center it exactly, and paste it to the square with rubber cement. Over this lay the third square of tracing paper, and make a clean, clear traced copy of your design (see Fig. 128); that is, include the border (both the edge and the inner line) and the lettering. Mark the center point too, but do *not* copy the straight lines that cross the plate.

On this fresh design sheet use the center point to mark with your compass a penciled circle with a 3-inch diameter. (See Fig. 129.) Do not scribe this circle on your silver when you do the rest of your design. Just leave it on your design sheet for later use with your mold. Put this square aside for the moment.

Step 5

Now lay the last of the 5-inch squares of tracing paper on the original design sheet. Trace *only* the outer edge of the plate on this square. Remove it from the design, and go over the edge you have just drawn, with pen and ink. (See Fig. 130.) Be very sure that the curves you have drawn are smooth and accurate. Now paste your square of tracing paper with this single line of design on it on to the square of silver. Be sure to use only rubber cement for this. The outline in pen and ink is to help you see clearly the line you are to cut with the jeweler's saw. When you have finished the cutting the paper can be easily removed and the rubber cement will rub right off with the fingers.

Step 6

Prepare the jeweler's saw as described in Chapter 5, and cut carefully along the curved edge. Remember at the sharp V's in the design to hold your saw upright in the same spot and continue to saw as you turn your piece. Pivot the silver, but hold the saw in the same place, with the smooth back part of the blade against the work already cut. This gives you a chance to cut almost down to the deep angles between curves. As before, leave the deepest part to be taken down with the needle files. (See Fig. 131.)

Step 7

When the curves are all cut, examine them carefully for any deviation from the line. These can be corrected by filing back to the line with the jeweler's half-round or triangular file.

Fig. 128
Making a fresh design
sheet

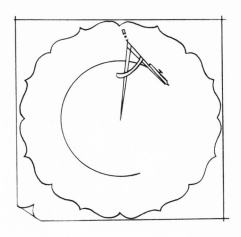

Fig. 129
Marking 3-inch circle for
shaping

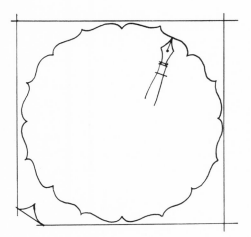

Fig. 130
Inking in cutting guide

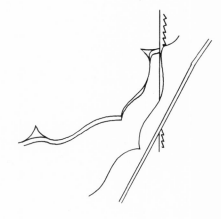

Fig. 131
Do not cut deeply between
scallops

Steps 8–13

Tear off the tracing paper that was your edge guide, and rub off the rubber cement. Taking the same precautions called for in Chapter 5, bevel the curved edges with the needle files and steel wool. Clean the silver with steel wool, paint with white tempera, cut a carbon sheet to fit, lay over it your clean design sheet, and transfer the entire design (name and inner border) to your plate. Do not transfer the 3-inch circle yet. Scribe your design as usual and follow the usual procedure in cleaning your plate, cleaning the back very well, painting it with asphaltum, turning it over on a double sheet of newsprint. Clean the front again before painting the design with asphaltum.

On a plate such as this, with a delicate border and an equally delicate type of lettering, the asphaltum painting must be exceptionally well done, with clean-painted edges. You will need to be particularly careful about covering every part of the curved rim, with its deep V's, with a smooth layer of asphaltum. Carry the paint at least ¼ inch beyond the edge onto the paper, as in previous painting, and let it dry overnight.

Step 14

You are now ready to etch your plate. Follow exactly the directions for etching silver in Chapter 5. When the etching is complete, clean and polish it as usual.

Step 15

You are now ready to mold your plate. Lay your clean pattern over the carbon paper circle that fitted it on your plate, and trace the 3-inch circle in the middle. (See Fig. 132.) Do not scribe it; just leave the carbon circle.

For the shaping of this plate, use the mold with the 3-inch hollow that was used for the shaping of the copper tea plate in Chapter 2, and follow all directions as they were given. Your carbon-marked circle gives you the placement of the hollow; do not make the indentation too deep.

Step 16

Oxidize, polish to highlight. A good silver polish used on the parts not oxidized can emphasize the design, if you wish, and a light buffing with a soft cloth will enhance it.

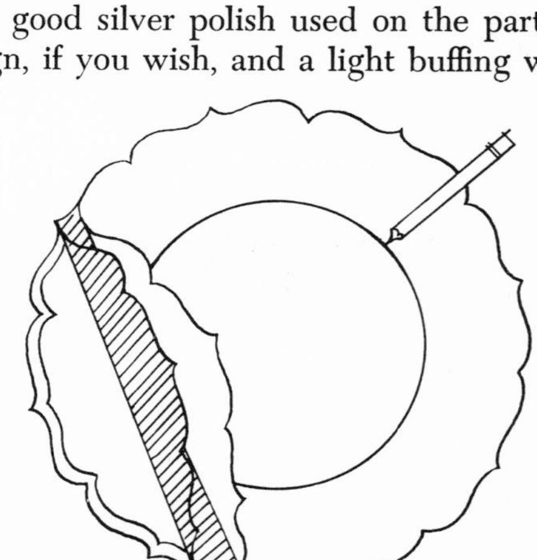

Fig. 132
Transferring 3-inch circle for shaping from design sheet to Plate

Chapter 7

CHILD'S SILVER BIB-CLIPS

THIS CHAPTER AND CHAPTER 8 CARRY INSTRUCTIONS FOR SOFT SOLDERING, sufficient for attaching pins, earrings, and clips.

In addition to materials on hand, you will need, to begin:

1 piece of silver, 1¼ x 1¾ inches (20-gauge)
1 very small glass dish; a glass ash tray will do
soft solder flux
soft solder wire
1 small brush (artist's #2) for flux
1 small pliers (flat-nosed and needle-nosed)
1 alcohol torch and denatured alcohol or denatured solvent

1 pair long-nosed tweezers
5 inches of sterling silver chain and 2 small links for connecting the chain
2 dress clip-backs (bought at handicraft supply store)
1 center punch
1 light hammer
clean nitric acid or fresh silver mordant
1 lb. yellow ochre
1 asbestos pad

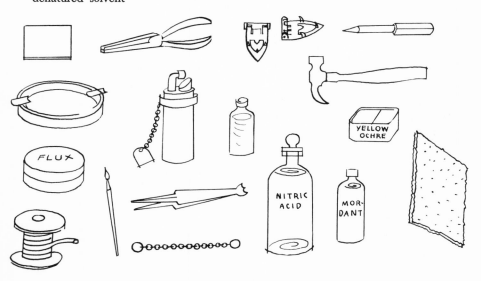

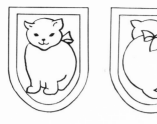

Fig. 133
Design drawn to exact size

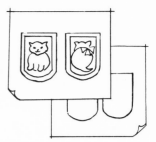

Fig. 134
Tracings, one with design,
one with outline only

Step 1

Decide on your design, either within this shape frame or some other shape you prefer. If you decide to use this design, trace it exactly as it is drawn to size. (See Fig. 133.) If you prefer to look for other designs, you will find children's books a rich source to tap.

Step 2

Make two tracings of each clip; on one trace the design, on the other only the outline, darkened by pen and ink. (See Fig. 134.)

Step 3

With rubber cement, paste onto your piece of silver the tracings that contain *only outlines*. (See Fig. 135.)

Fig. 135
Pasting pattern for cutting
edge on the silver with
rubber cement

Fig. 136
Placing the Clip in position
it will take

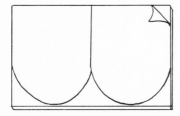

Step 4

Cut as closely as possible with the tinsnips and finish with the jeweler's saw, or cut entirely with the jeweler's saw.

Step 5

Bevel edges with half-round needle file and steel wool.

Step 6

Cut carbon paper to the size of the silver and have your clean copy of the design, also cut to size, ready to lay on the carbon.

Step 7

Clean and paint the silver with white tempera; when dry, clip on the prepared carbon and design sheets.

Steps 8, 9, 10

Follow the usual process in tracing, scribing, and painting in asphaltum back and front, and dry overnight.

You are now ready to etch your bib-clips. A small glass dish or a glass ash tray is enough for this.

Step 11

Follow exact directions given in Chapter 5 for etching with silver mordant, and in Chapter 2 for etching in general, with mordant or acid.

Step 12

When your etch has reached the desired depth, remove, rinse in cold water, and clean your pieces as usual, with turpentine and steel wool.

You are now ready to solder the clips to the back of your silver. Have your soldering materials ready and a bowl of cold water at hand before you begin

Step 13

These clip-backs are ¾ inch and should be centered on the back of the bib-clips ¼ inch from the top. (See Fig. 136.) Measure and mark the spot on your silver pieces.

Fig. 137
Clean area for soldering

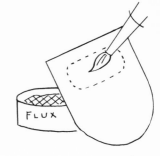

Fig. 138
Spreading flux

Step 14

Clean a small area on and around the spot to which the clip will be soldered. (See Fig. 137.) Solder will not adhere to uncleaned metal. Therefore do not clean the entire back; the part you leave uncleaned will keep your solder within bounds.

Step 15

Use paste flux, sold specifically for soft soldering. Spread it immediately over the cleaned spots with a small artist's paint brush. (See Fig. 138.)

Step 16

Try to get a solid wire solder. However, if that is unobtainable, use an acid core solder. Hammer flat about ½ inch of one end of the solder on a metal surface. (See Fig. 139.) (Use the back of your iron frying pan.)

Step 17

With a scissors, cut the end into thin slivers like fringe. Then cut these slivers crossways once or twice over a saucer to catch the tiny bits of solder. (See Fig. 140.)

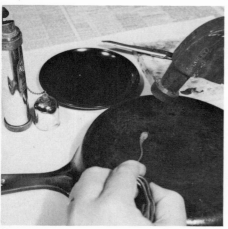

Fig. 139
Flattening solder before cutting

Fig. 140
Cutting fine bits of solder

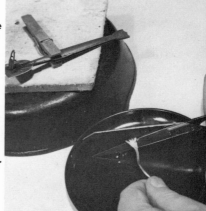

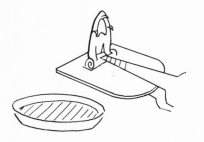

Fig. 141
Holding Clip in place with
tweezers

Step 18

Lay your silver piece face-down on an asbestos pad. Lay the clip-back
on the fluxed spot and hold it in place with a pair of long-nosed tweezers that
have been dipped at the tip up to ½ inch into a yellow ochre paste. (See
Fig. 141.) This is prepared by mixing about ¼ teaspoon of yellow ochre in
enough water to make a creamy paste. The yellow ochre keeps the tweezers
free from solder. It is very cheap and is sold by all craft supply houses. You
use little at a time; 1 lb. will last a long while.

Step 19

After the clip-back is held in place with your tweezers, make sure that the
movable part of the clip is upright out of the way. Fasten your tweezers in
position with a spring clothespin. This frees both hands for work. (See
Fig. 142.)

Step 20

With your brush moistened with the flux, pick up and place four bits of
the cut solder around the narrow strip to be soldered to the silver. (See
Fig. 142.) Remember, be careful to keep the flux and bits of solder off the
movable part lest the solder fasten it in place.

Fig. 142
Placing solder around base
of Clip

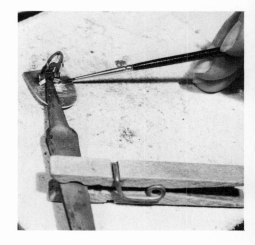

Fig. 143
Ready for soldering with
an alcohol burner

Fig. 144
Cooling all units after
soldering

Step 21

Light your alcohol burner, after filling it according to the manufacturer's directions. (See Fig. 143.) Apply your heat at first everywhere on the metal except on your solder and clip-back. You will notice that your flux melts almost immediately. Shortly after, your solder will begin to flow. At this moment, transfer your flame directly to the clip. This will bring the clip-back up to the temperature of your silver and will draw the solder in between the two metals. It will show like a silver line at the edge. When that happens, remove your heat and blow out your torch.

Step 22

With a teaspoon, pour a small amount of cold water over the soldered joint. This hardens the solder but does not cool the silver sufficiently. With a pair of pliers now pick up your piece (tweezers included) and dip it in your bowl of water. (See Fig. 144.) It is immediately cool enough to handle.

You will now need:

1 twist drill #60 bit (you already have a drill handle)
1 center punch

Fig. 146
Marking, with center punch,
point to be pierced

Fig. 145
Marking, with pencil, point
to be pierced

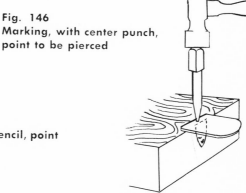

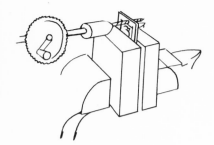

Fig. 147
Piercing silver to attach
chain

Step 23

Dry your silver pieces thoroughly. Mark with a pencil the center of the top border, equi-distant from each end. (See Fig. 145.) The hole for the chain is to be drilled at this point. Because of the clip on the back, the silver cannot be laid flat on the table; it must be laid over the edge of a thick piece of scrap wood to mark the penciled point with a center punch. (See Fig. 146.) (It would have been simpler to pierce the hole before the soldering, but you take the chance of the solder running into the hole and plugging it.)

To hold the silver pieces for piercing, set them upright in the vise protected from the jaws of the vise by a piece of wood on either side, as shown in Fig. 147. Make sure that the movable spring of the clip is out of the way. Attach your #60 drill bit to your hand-drill. Drill one hole in each piece of silver on the marked point, drilling from the front to the back. (See Fig. 147.) The hole must be drilled as close to the top of the silver as possible without breaking the edge; therefore place the end of your drill against the border to get a better picture of the space you need. Let this be your guide. However, if you are using larger links to connect the chain to the silver piece, you can place your hole a little farther from the edge.

Step 24

Remove the silver pieces from the vise and run a flat or oval needle file across the back part of each hole to remove the burr left from the cutting. (See Fig. 148.)

You are now ready to attach the chain.

Fig. 148
Filing off the burr after
drilling

Step 25

Hold the large link with a pair of pliers at each tip so that you can look through the loop. Separate the ends of the loop by moving one pair of pliers toward you and the other away .(See Fig. 149.) Slip the loop through the drilled hole and place the end link of the chain over the open end of the loop. Now close the loop by reversing the process by which you opened it. Repeat this process on the other link and bib-clip, fastening it to the other end of the 5-inch silver chain. Polish and oxidize and polish again to highlight. Use silver polish if desired.

Later, these clips can be worn as a dress decoration, with or without a chain.

Made in larger sizes with heavier chains and back clips, these can be used as baby blanket holders. Another variation makes an attractive gift for an adult: silver name-plates for decanters with both ends of the chain caught in the one decorative piece of silver will be an interesting project for you to make and an impressive gift for a friend to receive.

Yet another gift might be a set of small silver charms on each of which is etched the name and birthdate of a grandchild, to fasten to a "Grandmother Bracelet." Charms to attach to a girl's bracelet, or an interesting medallion as a fob decoration for a boy, with designs to follow their interests are good gifts to consider. The figure of a ballerina, a baseball player, or a crossed tennis racquet and baseball bat, would make appropriate designs, not difficult to plan and execute.

Fig. 149
Attaching chain

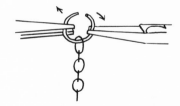

Chapter 8

PIN AND EARRING SET—NICKEL SILVER ON COPPER

IN ADDITION TO THE MATERIALS ON HAND, YOU WILL NEED, TO BEGIN:

1 piece of Tu-Tone metal, 2 x 3½ inches (copper, plated with nickel silver) see back of book for supplier

1 pin back, 2½ inches long, and clasp (mounted on disks)
1 pair earring backs

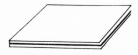

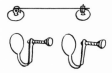

This metal comes in 6 x 6 inches and larger sizes and may be bought in "bracelet strips" up to 1½ inches in width. The actual amount needed for this pin and earring set is 2 x 3½ inches. If it cannot be bought in a "bracelet strip," it must be cut from the larger piece with tinsnips. The pin is 2 x 2¾ inches; the earrings ½ x ¾ inches. (See Fig. 150.) These earrings were made smaller than usual because of the personal taste of the recipient, but a pin of this size could take a pair of earrings of 1 x ¾ inches, which would cut out exactly from the 2 x 3½-inch piece of metal. (See two sizes of earrings in Fig. 151.)

Fig. 150
Plan for cutting pieces from larger piece of metal

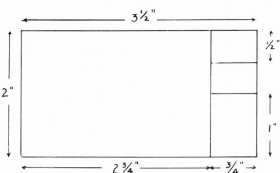

Fig. 151
Pin and two Earring sizes
to be traced

Step 1

Cut the copper to the size of the pin and earrings. Prepare your design as usual. If you wish to trace this, draw it exactly to size. (See Fig. 151.) Whichever size you choose for earrings, be sure to reverse the design for its mate. This particular design was traced from a newspaper advertisement of a tray. As it was the required size, it was traced with only a slight change in design. The earrings were adapted from the pin.

Steps 2–8

Bevel the edges and clean the surface. The nickel silver side will be the side on which the design is placed. The acid will cut away the nickel silver and leave the copper around the silver design. Nickel is much harder than either copper or sterling silver. Therefore, in scribing your design, it will be necessary to press harder in order to leave an imprint strong enough to work by with the asphaltum. Follow all steps as in Chapter 2 and etch as usual. Nickel silver can be etched in the same etching bath as copper pieces, and it works exactly like copper. Etch this only in copper mordant or nitric acid solution—never in silver mordant.

Step 9

After the pin and earrings are cleaned with turpentine, following the etch, you are ready to solder on the pin, its clasp, and the earring backs.
Prepare for soldering as in Chapter 7.

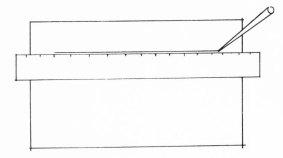

Fig. 152
Marking level for soldering
Pin

Step 10

Scribe a ruled line across the back of your pin ⅝ of an inch from the top, starting and ending at ¼ inch from each side. (See Fig. 152.) The easiest kind of pin backs to attach are those that are already mounted on ¼-inch disks of metal. Place the two disks of your pin back and catch so that the outer edge of the disk reaches the ¼ inch mark from each side, and mark their placement with a dot of your scriber. (See Fig. 153.) Remove the pin and catch and clean well with steel wool on the spots where your pin and catch are to be attached. Immediately put flux on the cleaned spots. Clean the back of the disks with steel wool and put flux on each at once.

Fig. 153
Placing Pin and disks in
position

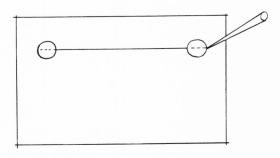

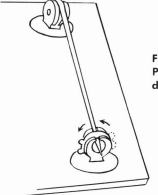

Fig. 154
Pin closed with safety clasp
downward

Step 11

Set the pin in the catch and close the safety clasp so that it faces down-ward. (See Fig. 154.) By doing this you are keeping pin and clasp in line and assuring the full usefulness of your safety clasp. Replace the pin and catch on the metal. Make sure that the pin point extends through the clasp and a little beyond. Clip the tweezers over the pinbar and the etched piece itself, so as to anchor both clasp and pin disks for the entire soldering opera-tion. (See Fig. 155.) Cut solder as described in Chapter 7. With your flux brush slip two pieces of cut solder under each disk spot. (See Fig. 156.)

Fig. 155
Holding Pin bar with tweezer in position for soldering

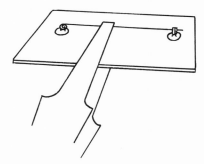

Fig. 156
Applying solder

Step 12

Light the alcohol burner and follow previous soldering instructions. Be careful never to apply heat directly to the long pin. Direct flame will soften the pin and make it difficult to put through the material of a dress. In this, you will see the solder run like a silver line around the *outside* of the rim of each disk when it is ready. At that point apply your flame momentarily to the two disks to bring them up to proper temperature. Remove your flame and quench it. Pour a little water on each disk from a spoon, then lift the etched pin, tweezers included, and plunge it into water to cool. Examine the pin point; if it extends beyond the edge of your metal, clip the extra length off with a cutting pliers. (see Fig. 157), and sharpen the point with a file. If your pin seems slightly tight in the clasp, file it a little thinner on all sides so that it moves readily in and out of the clasp and the safety closes well over it.

Fig. 157
Cutting off extra length of Pin

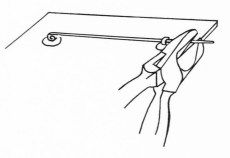

Fig. 158
Soldering Earring backs

Step 13

You are now ready to solder the earring backs.

Making earrings affords an opportunity to suit the personality of the wearer; often they are made more comfortable and becoming by the correct placement of the earring back. Therefore try earrings on the wearer-to-be before soldering; then mark for placement.

Soldering earring backs follows the exact procedure for pin backs, except for placing four pieces of solder under the disks before holding them in place with the tweezers. (These earring backs have a slightly larger disk than the pin clasps.) Unscrew the earring backs to make the widest opening, to prevent soldering them closed by accident. Follow directions as in soldering the pin. (See Fig. 158.)

Step 14

Polish all three pieces, oxidize, polish again with steel wool. Spray with lacquer if desired.

Chapter 9

SILVER POWDER SCOOP—
SILVER SALT SPOONS

A SMALL SILVER SCOOP IN A POWDER BOX OR JAR CAN BE SURPRISINGLY convenient for filling a compact and eliminating the annoyance of spilled powder on polished surfaces. It makes a charming small gift, takes a fairly short time to fashion, and is not expensive. It is very good-looking in copper also, at a very slight cost.

The silver salt spoons are exactly the same as the scoop, but smaller. Sizes are given in exact diagrams.

In addition to the materials on hand, you will need, to begin:

For the scoop:
    1 piece of 20-gauge sterling silver, 3¼ x 1⅝ inches
    1 piece of cardboard
For the salt spoons:
    1 piece 20-gauge sterling silver 2⅛ x ⅞ inches for one spoon or
    1 piece 20-gauge sterling silver 3¼ x 6⅞ inches for set of six spoons

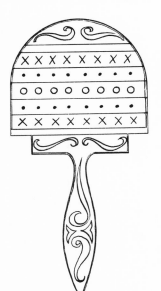

Fig. 159
Powder Scoop exact size

Fig. 160
Salt Spoon exact size

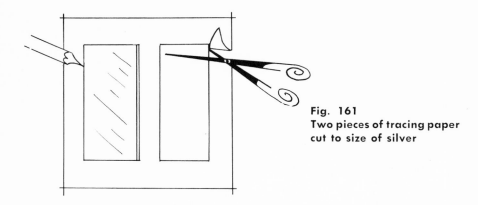

Fig. 161
Two pieces of tracing paper
cut to size of silver

Step 1

Outline your 3¼ x 1⅝-inch piece of silver on tracing paper. Cut two copies. On each piece trace the outline of the scoop, which is drawn to exact size. (See Fig. 161.)

Step 2

On one tracing go over the line with pen and ink; this will be pasted on the silver for the edge cutting, and the other will be used to transfer the *design* of the scoop. (See Fig. 162.)

Step 3

With carbon paper, transfer the pattern to the cardboard and cut it out with sharp scissors. Lay this aside; it will be used for duplicate copies or for the making of several scoops at once, if needed.

Step 4

With rubber cement, paste down the ink-lined tracing on the piece of silver. (See Fig. 163.)

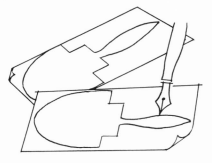

Fig. 162
Trace one outline in ink

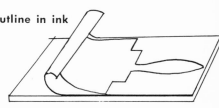

Fig. 163
Pasting inked outline on silver for cutting

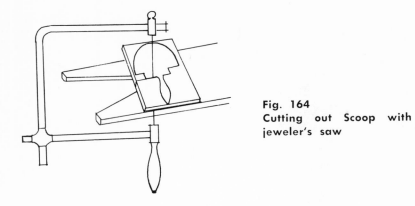

Fig. 164
Cutting out Scoop with
jeweler's saw

Step 5

Cut carefully along the inked line with the jeweler's saw. (See Fig. 164.) Remove the tracing paper and rub the cut-out scoop with the fingers to clear the silver of rubber cement.

Step 6

Examine Fig. 165. You will find two cut-out edges marked A-B, B-C and D-E, E-F. Do *not* bevel these edges, but *do* bevel the rest of the scoop and the handle, using the triangular or the half-round jeweler's file. (See dotted areas in Fig. 165.) Remember: silver is softer than copper. Work lightly, from both faces of the metal as usual, alternating with the fine steel wool.

Fig. 165
Dotted lines to be beveled
as usual

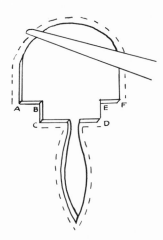

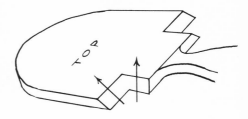

Fig. 166
Angle of filing for corner mitre

Fig. 167
Finished angles of all four corner surfaces

Step 7

On the edges marked A-B, B-C and D-E, E-F, file only on one face of the scoop, to an angle of 45°. (See Figs. 166 and 167.) This allows for a close joining of the corners when the scoop is shaped. (See Fig. 173.)

Step 8

Now prepare your design. You have on hand the second piece of tracing paper on which you drew the outline of the scoop in Step 2. If you wish to use the design that is given in Fig. 159, it is full size, and can be traced directly on to your design sheet.

Step 9

Cut out the tracing paper with the design filled in, to the shape of the cut-out scoop. Cut a piece of carbon paper to match. (See Fig. 168.) Clean and paint the silver piece with white tempera as usual and allow it to dry.

Fig. 168
Design sheet and carbon paper cut to shape of silver

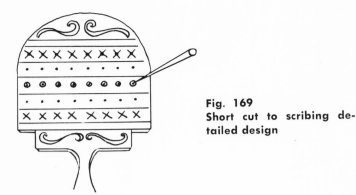

Fig. 169
Short cut to scribing detailed design

Step 10

Lay your design sheet over the carbon paper on your silver and anchor them down with paper fasteners. Three are plenty. In transferring the design, draw in first the *division lines* of the design, the thin border, and the *curves* at the top and bottom of the scoop and on the handle. You will notice that the designs *between* the lines are merely crosses, dots, and small circles. Instead of marking in these small figures, it is better to make a dot in the center of each to mark the placement. (See Fig. 169.) When you are painting with asphaltum, you will find it easier to mark in the small figures freehand over each dot than to follow the marks scribed in completely.

Step 11

Make sure that you have traced in all lines and placement dots. Remove the design sheet and carbon and scribe through the white tempera. Wash off the white tempera, as usual. You are now ready to clean and paint your scoop with asphaltum.

Fig. 170
Painting design freehand following scribed dots

Fig. 171
First step in shaping Powder
Scoop over wood block

Fig. 172
Completing shaping of side
of Powder Scoop on wood
block

Step 12

Clean and paint the back of the scoop and turn it on newsprint as usual.
Set up the design sheet before you, so that you can refer to it at all times
while painting the design on the scoop. (See Fig. 170.)

Step 13

Clean the front of the scoop and paint the curved bands at the top and the
first dividing band across. Then paint in the line of crosses free-hand, letting
the two small lines of each cross at the scribed dot. (See Fig. 170.) Continue with the alternate lines painted in asphaltum across the scoop, with
the crosses, dots, and circles between. When the curved bands near the
handle and on the handle itself are painted in, paint in the narrow border all
around the edge of the scoop. Check carefully and make sure that the ends
of the crosses or the edges of the dots or circles do *not* touch the bands that
cross the scoop or the border at any point. Keep all units of the design clearly
free of each other. Scratch a line with your scriber to separate any asphaltum
that touches where it should not. Paint the border out onto the paper to
protect the edge, as usual.

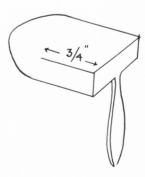

Fig. 173
Completed bowl of Powder
Scoop

Step 14

Etch to a fairly deep etch (⅓ of the thickness of the metal) in silver mordant or 3 to 1 nitric acid.

With your scoop etched and cleaned you are ready to shape it. You will now need:

1 light hammer
1 oval dapping tool—(oval end Dixon S-2144)
    or a similar tool from any other supply house
1 lead block (about 4 x 4 x 1 inches)
1 piece of hardwood 1 x 1 x 3 inches

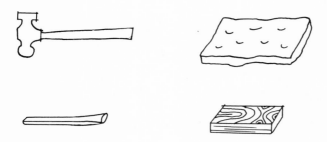

Step 15

Set the piece of 1-inch thick hardwood in the vise, projecting up about two inches (as it appears in Fig. 171). Set the scoop face down on the wood so that the cut-out corners reach the edge of the wood. Holding the scoop firmly down to the top of the wood, tap one side of the silver with the mallet, starting from the square corner and working ¾ of an inch toward the front curve, until the tapped section is flat against the side of the wood block. (See Fig. 171.) Then tap over the other side edge on the wood block for the same ¾ inch. Finally, tap back the handle section until the cut edges of silver meet. (See Figs. 172 and 173.) You do not tap the long sides more than ¾ inch from the corner joining; it is more attractive to have the line of the scoop flaring a bit at the front.

Now your scoop is shaped and you are ready to shape the handle. You must prepare a hollow for this.

Fig. 174
Outlining shape of Scoop
handle on lead block

Fig. 175
Preparing hollow in lead
block for molding Scoop
handle

Step 16

Lay the lead block at the edge of the table, and lay the handle of the scoop across the middle of the block. Outline on the lead block, with your scriber, the handle of your scoop. (See Fig. 174.) Within the shape you have drawn, slide the oval dapping tool, with a rocking motion, tapping the tool with the hammer as you move it back and forth. (See Fig. 175.) You are thus making a hollow deeper in the middle, shallower at the two ends. (See Fig. 176.) This has formed a mold in which to shape your scoop handle.

Step 17

Lay the scoop handle, etched side down, over the depression you have made in the lead block. Place your dapping tool in the middle of the handle and move it up and down its length, tapping lightly and continuously with the hammer on the upper end of the dapping tool. You will find that the handle curves up at both sides and at the tip. (See Fig. 177.) The dapping has given the handle the proper sweep; all that remains to be done is to bend the handle back slightly by hand where it joins the bowl of the scoop. (See Fig. 178.) Polish, oxidize, and polish again.

Fig. 177
Shaping curve of Scoop
handle with dapping tool
on lead block

Fig. 176
Cross section of hollow

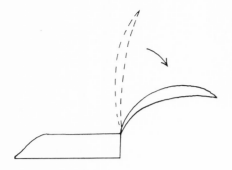

Fig. 178
Bend shaped handle back
by hand to proper angle

In a smaller size this makes an excellent salt spoon, and two or more make a fine gift. A pattern of the smaller scoop is given in Fig. 160 at the beginning of this chapter. The salt spoons are made in exactly the same way as the powder scoop. It is an economy of material to make more than one, since the pattern for each can be laid out as in Fig. 179. Make a cardboard pattern as in Step 3 of the scoop to help you lay out and plan the alternate up and down placement of the salt spoons.

The finished powder scoop, well-polished, oxidized, and polished again, is very attractive placed on a ½-inch thickness of absorbent cotton, fastened across with a green ribbon, and placed in a small plastic box. (See Fig. 180.) In boxing the salt spoons, lay them alternately up and down in the box, or side by side, depending on the number in the gift.

This scoop has been used to good effect as a nut scoop.

If it is made in copper, polish the finished scoop, oxidize and polish it again, and lacquer it with colorless nail polish.

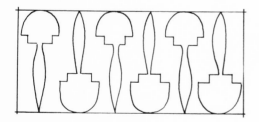

Fig. 179
Economy in cutting silver
for set of Salt Spoons

Fig. 180
Suggested gift-packaging
of Powder Scoop in plastic
box

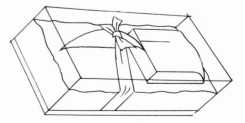

Fig. 181
Actual size of design of Bracelet

98

Chapter 10

A SHAPED SILVER BRACELET

THIS PROJECT IN STERLING SILVER IS VERY BEAUTIFUL. IN COPPER, PROPERLY oxidized and polished, it is equally handsome and makes a good-looking and inexpensive gift.

In addition to the materials on hand, you will now need, to begin:

1 piece of 20-gauge sterling silver 2¾ x 7¼ inches
    or
1 piece of copper (18-gauge) 2¾ x 7¼ inches

Step 1

The pattern given here is the whole bracelet, in the actual size. (See Fig. 181.) Trace the outline on firm tracing paper and cut out two copies, (See Fig. 182.) Lay one piece of tracing paper on the design (Fig. 181) and trace it exactly.

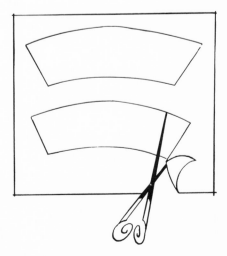

Fig. 182
Two sheets of tracing paper
cut to size

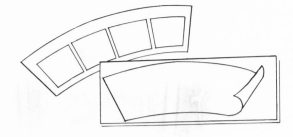

Fig. 183
Inked outline—no design—
pasted on silver for cutting

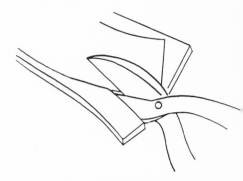

Fig. 184
One method of cutting out
silver Bracelet

Step 2

Lay the tracing paper pattern without the design on the sheet of silver, as close to the edge as possible to avoid waste, and paste it down with rubber cement. (See Fig. 183.) Cut around this pattern on the silver with either tinsnips or the jeweler's saw, as in Chapter 5. (See Fig. 184.) Save the pieces of silver that are cut out around this pattern. They will make several jewelry pieces when you are ready.

Steps 3–5

Bevel all edges with files and steel wool after clearing off the tracing paper and rubber cement. For this sweep of edge, use the finer of your larger files, not the needle files. (See Fig. 185.) Lay carbon paper and the design sheet (cut to size) over the white-painted silver and transfer the design in pencil as usual.

Note the design of this bracelet. It seems complicated, but it is not. Except for the four central designs, which are identical motifs and not difficult to paint in asphaltum, the lines with simple crosses and brush marks between are almost the same as in the powder scoop. Actually we are using simple forms to achieve an effect that is rich and intricate in appearance. (See detail of design.) In using the scriber to mark the design on the tempera-painted silver, it is not necessary to mark every line of the small units of the design. First, just scribe the dividing lines across the bracelet, the central motifs, the dividing lines between, and the fine border around the whole piece.

Fig. 185
Beveling with large fine file

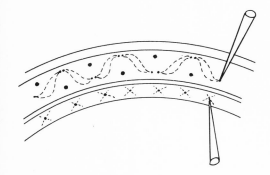

Fig. 186
Scribing dots for painting
in asphaltum of small de-
sign units

For the smaller units a scratched dot at the necessary intervals will assure
proper spacing by marking the middle of each cross; each line is a simple
brush stroke crossing the dot. (See Fig. 186.) Be careful not to have the
edges of the crosses touch the dividing lines separating the design. The
upper row of the design we call "hither and return." In scribing that, if you
prefer, simply scribe dots to indicate start and finish of the curved lines. (See
letter *A* in Figure 187.) When you paint in asphaltum, you make the curved
brush strokes between the dots. (See letter *B* in Figure 187.) Again be careful not to have the edges of these brush strokes touch the dividing lines you
have painted across your design—*C* and *D* in Fig. 187.

Fig. 187
Developing design from
guidance dots

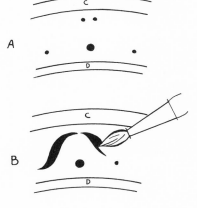

Fig. 188
Shaping Bracelet around
tumbler

Step 6

Make sure that the back of your piece is well protected by the asphaltum and, after it has been placed on the newsprint, paint in the four motifs, the borders and the dividing lines across the bracelet. With the rest of the units painted in, see that all edges have been well painted for protection. You are now ready to let your piece dry overnight and etch it.

Step 7

Follow directions for etching silver in either silver mordant, copper mordant, or nitric acid, as given in Chapters 2 and 5, depending on whether the bracelet is being made in copper or silver.

This piece of silver fits into an 8-inch square container, or you may own a relish dish that will serve. Try it out first for size. Etch to approximately ⅓ of the thickness of your silver.

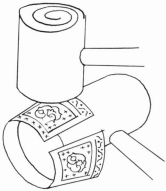

Fig. 189
Finishing shaping Bracelet
around mallet

Step 8

When your bracelet is etched and cleaned, you are ready to shape it for wearing. Find a glass or metal tumbler that is a little wider at the top than at the base. Use this to help you bend the bracelet to shape.

Hold the middle of the bracelet against the glass and gradually press the ends of the silver around it. (See Fig. 188.) The ends should touch. Transfer your shaped bracelet from the glass to the head of your round-nosed mallet and tap it with your buckskin mallet against the rounded wood. (See Fig. 189.) Tap each end in turn on the wooden mallet, so that when the bracelet is worn, it is slightly oval in shape and will follow the same smooth curve on the wrist. (See Fig. 190.)

Step 9

Polish and oxidize. In a design such as this, you can try some interesting effects in oxidizing. Try darkening the four motifs and the edges, top and bottom, and graduating the lightness in between. If you don't care for the effect, clean it off well with steel wool, oxidize again, and try the emphasis elsewhere on the design. It is on a good-looking piece such as this, in a size easy to handle, that you can work out effects in highlighting and emphasizing a design by care in oxidizing. You can then apply this method in the handling of larger projects that come later. Polish your piece to finish.

If this is made in copper, paint the inside of the bracelet with colorless nail polish to prevent it from discoloring the wrist. If you prefer, spray the entire bracelet with lacquer, after you are sure that it is oxidized and polished exactly to your liking.

Fig. 190
Bracelet finished in slightly
oval shape to fit wrist

104

Chapter 11

COPPER PLATES

Part 1. 12-inch Circular Plate in Copper

In ADDITION TO THE MATERIALS ON HAND, YOU WILL NEED FOR THE 12-INCH plate, to begin:

1 12-inch disk of 18-gauge copper (this size can be bought ready cut)
1 12-inch mold with a hollow of 9, 10, or 11 inches

Step 1

Bevel the edges of your copper as usual. (See Fig. 191.)

Fig. 191

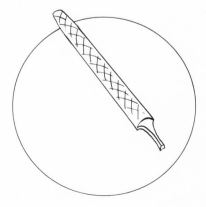

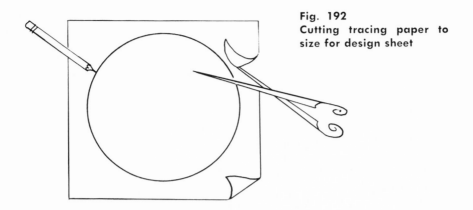

Fig. 192
Cutting tracing paper to
size for design sheet

Step 2

Mark and cut out your tracing paper and carbon paper to the size of the copper. (See Fig. 192.)

There is no formal design here to be traced or worked out. This design is made by drops of asphaltum from your medium-sized brush, dropped at intervals on your copper plate. (It is described in detail further on.)

Step 3

Get the center of the paper circle by folding it exactly in half, then refolding in half again. (See Fig. 193.) The point of crossed creases is the center.

Step 4

Use this point with your compass and draw an 11-inch circle on your sheet. This will form a ½-inch border. (See Fig. 194.)

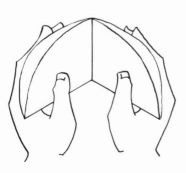

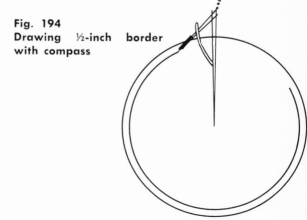

Fig. 194
Drawing ½-inch border
with compass

Fig. 193
Folding paper circle to find
center

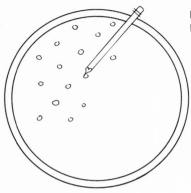

Fig. 195
Drawing dots at random

Fig. 196
Indicating location of dots
with half-circles

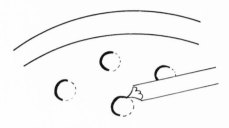

Step 5

Then draw dots at random over the entire sheet within the border. Keep to about the same distance (from 1 inch to 1¼ inches) from each other, but do not attempt to keep in line in any direction. (See Fig. 195.) When your design sheet is filled with dots, glance over it and correct any impression of either crowding or lack, by erasing a dot or adding another where needed. When the dots are placed to your satisfaction, draw a slight crescent to the side of each dot. (See Fig. 196.) You are now ready to transfer this design through the carbon to the prepared white-painted copper.

Step 6

Do *not* mark the dot through the carbon. After marking your border, trace only the crescents onto the plate. These half-circles and the border will be all that will be scribed on the plate. The reason for scribing the half-circles will be understood when you paint in the dots of the asphaltum. (See Fig. 197.)

Fig. 197
Compare design sheet with
finished Plate

Fig. 198
Beginning an asphaltum
dot

Fig. 199
Brush tip held on spot to
control size

Step 7

Clean and prepare your plate thoroughly as usual. When the front of your plate is ready to paint, you have only the border and the dots to do. Do the dots first.

Step 8

Before you paint the front of your plate, you will find it helpful to practice painting the dots on scrap copper. Clean the piece of scrap copper on which you are going to experiment. Scribe several crescents the size of those you have used in your design. Use your medium brush, fill it with asphaltum, and hold it over the jar till one full drop goes back into the jar. Then touch your copper a little to the side of a crescent within its curve. (See Fig. 198.) The asphaltum spot will be small, so keep your brush tip just touching the middle of this spot for a second. (See Fig. 199.) Then lift. The amount of asphaltum on your brush, plus the time you hold your brush, controls the size of the dot. The asphaltum dot should spread to touch the crescent. You will find that the knack of controlling the size comes quickly with practice. Do not attempt to paint in a larger dot than one that is dropped. Do not try to make the dots identical. If a dot is much too small, drop a tiny bit more asphaltum on the center of it, but wherever possible do not try to correct any dot by painting it larger with brush strokes. Wipe it off with turpentine if you must, clean the spot with steel wool, and continue.

Step 9

When you have practiced enough (which will be very soon), follow the same method on your plate. After that, you will find that it is easy to paint the border. Protect the edge well and leave it to dry. Etch as usual in copper mordant, or 3 to 1 nitric acid.

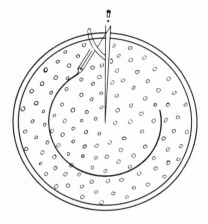

**Fig. 200
Marking in pencil for shaping etched Plate**

Step 10

Containers for etching of this size plate are discussed at the end of this chapter. After etching, clean and prepare to shape your plate.

Step 11

To shape this plate a 12-inch mold with a 9-inch hollow was used. It could be shaped on a mold with a 10-, 11-, or 12-inch hollow. In a 12-inch hollow, with no rim, and double handles, this is very effective also. Lay your pattern for a moment on your copper circle; using the point of your compass or your scriber, mark the center you have there, through the paper to the copper. Then using your compass draw a 9-inch circle in pencil directly on your 12-inch plate to match the hollow in the mold. (See Fig. 200.) This circle will be easy to center as the rim exactly fits the circular mold. If your mold is square, pencil the circle of your plate on the rim of the mold to guide you. Then hammer, as described in Chapters 2, 4, and 6, with your round-nosed wooden mallet. (See Figs. 63, 64, and 65 in Chapter 2.) This will be somewhat more difficult because of its larger size, but if you remember (1) to overlap your strokes to keep a smooth rim, and (2) to turn your plate over to flatten the rim from time to time, and (3) not to go down completely into the hollow of the mold, you will find the results rewarding. Polish, oxidize, and polish again, as usual.

Part 2. A 13-inch Circular Plate with Handles

(See photo of finished plate on p. 104)

In addition to the materials on hand, you will now need:

1 13-inch square of copper, 18-gauge
2 pieces of copper, each ⅝ x 16 inches
4 ⅛-inch rivets, copper, ⅜ inches long
1 hammer
1 riveting hammer

1 pliers with a cutting edge
1 mold with a 12-inch hollow
1 piece of dowel #10 (⅝ inch in diameter) 4½ inches long
1 rivet set (optional)

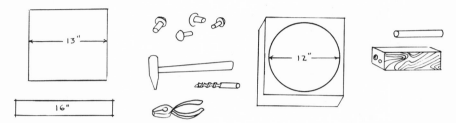

Copper does not come in die-cut disks of 13 inches, so it will be necessary to buy your copper in a sheet of the size you require.

Step 1

Use your dividers to mark a 13-inch circle on your 13-inch copper square. Cut it out with the tinsnips. (See Fig. 201.)

Step 2

Now take your strip of copper 1¾ x 16 inches and draw a line down the exact center, dividing it into two long strips ⅝ x 16 inches. Cut along this line with tinsnips. (See Fig. 202.) Lay these strips aside for your handles.

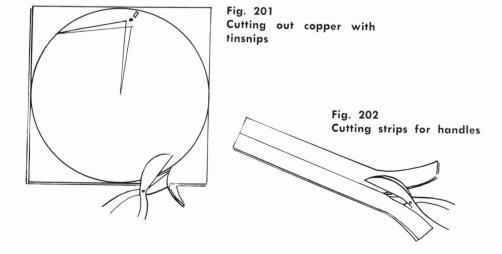

Fig. 201
Cutting out copper with tinsnips

Fig. 202
Cutting strips for handles

Fig. 203
Design of Plate—actual size

Fig. 204
Development of design

Fig. 205
Whole outer edge becomes border

Step 3

Bevel the edges of the copper circle as usual, and mark and cut to size the corresponding circles in tracing and carbon paper.

Step 4

If you wish to use this design, it is reproduced in actual size in Fig. 203.

This particular design was taken from wallpaper, simply traced and adapted slightly. (See Fig. 204.) Make sure that your design is traced and placed on the exact center of the 13-inch circle of paper which is your design sheet. This is very important, as the eye quickly detects a flaw in a placement of this sort. Paint your plate with tempera, trace, and scribe the design on it as usual. Paint with asphaltum as in previous projects. You will notice that the design takes up only 6 inches in the center of the plate. The large outer surface on the front of the plate, from the scallops bordering the design to the extreme edge, is solidly painted with asphaltum and forms the only border necessary. (See Fig. 205.)

Examine this carefully after it is painted, to make sure there are no spots that are too thinly painted and look reddish. If there are any thin spots, repaint over them. This smooth section must not be scarred by the entrance of any spot of acid or mordant. Protect the edges as usual, and dry overnight; etch in copper mordant or nitric acid as in Chapter 2. After etching, clean your plate and prepare to stipple the background of your design.

Step 5

You will now need:

3 or 4 nails, about 3 inches long
    a piece of iron or steel—use your iron frying pan, turned upside down

Stippling is used to add a pattern to the background of some designs (that is, to those parts around the design that have already been cut away by the acid). This background pattern holds the oxidizing and sharpens the effect of the highlighted design. It is a pitting of the copper done with an ordinary 2½-inch nail and hammer, and a coarse file to keep the nail sharpened. We use iron or steel to work on, as the hard metal keeps the copper from stretching out of shape too much in the stippling.

Turn your iron frying pan upside down on your work-bench or thickly padded table. Make sure that the handle extends over the edge to allow the iron pan to sit perfectly flat. On this, set your etched plate (see Fig. 206) design side up. Settle yourself comfortably at the table so that your elbows are resting on the table; your hands with a hammer in one and a nail in the other, are held over the design on your copper circle. If you wish, you can set the point of the nail on the copper between the design units, tap lightly with the hammer, move the nail, tap, and repeat until the background is covered by this pitted pattern. A quicker way, that makes a more interesting stipple, is to hold the nail between the thumb and forefinger of the left hand, with the point just above the surface of the copper but not touching it. (See Fig. 207.) Hold the nail lightly and tap it with the hammer, moving the nail slowly around above the part to be stippled. The vibrations of the nail as it

**Fig. 206
Etched Plate right side up
on iron frying pan**

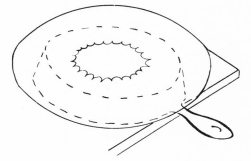

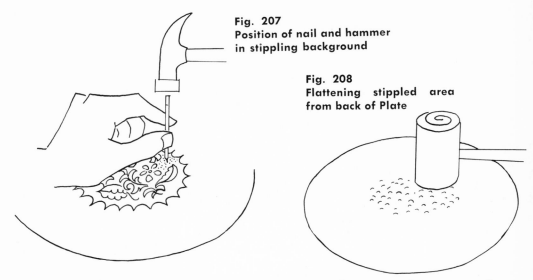

Fig. 207
Position of nail and hammer
in stippling background

Fig. 208
Flattening stippled area
from back of Plate

is moved and steadily tapped, make many marks, seemingly, at once; the pitting is more delicate, and the whole procedure is considerably speeded up. Working with the copper resting on the iron has kept it from stretching in the stippling, but turn the copper upside down occasionally on the floor or on the underside of a large solid mold, and strike it lightly with the buckskin mallet to make sure it stays flat. (See Fig. 208.)

Step 6

You are now ready to make the handles for the plate.

Bevel all edges of the two strips of copper and smooth them well with steel wool. Hammer lightly with your buckskin mallet to flatten and take out "kinks." Measure off 4½ inches on one copper strip. Slip the wooden dowel under it. (See Fig. 209.) Press the copper twice around the dowel at the angles shown in Fig. 210. Repeat for the other handle, working from the opposite direction to make a pair. (See Fig. 211.) The space between the ends will be wider than the length of the curled part of the handle and should meet the plate at 4 inches.

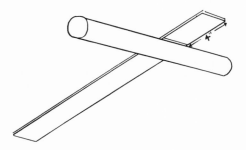

Fig. 209
Placement of dowel for first
step in turning handles

Fig. 210
Turning copper strip for handle

Step 7

You are now ready to shape your plate. Lay your design sheet on your copper plate and mark the center. With your compass, mark the 12-inch circle in pencil on your 13-inch plate. Then, using the larger mold with the 12-inch hollow, set your plate upon it and tap lightly and firmly within your 12-inch penciled circle. You will now have a ½-inch border to lie flat on the mold. This small rim must be watched to be kept as flat as the larger rims in other projects had to be. Lightly tap along the inside of the rim. The round-nosed wooden mallet should leave no scratch marks on the copper but should just mark the outline of the hollow. Try to keep an even stroke going around the rim till it has all been shaped to the mold. It is not necessary to hammer the middle. Do the sides just enough to suit the metal to the gentle slope of the mold. Do not make any more strokes than are necessary for shaping.

Fig. 211
Appearance of *pair* of handles when turned. *B* is turned in opposite direction to *A*

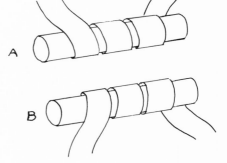

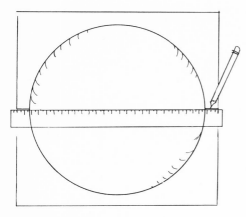

Fig. 212
Drawing center line on mold

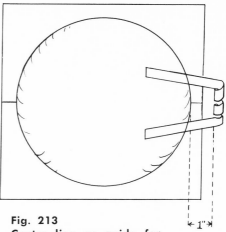

Fig. 213
Center line as guide for placing handles

←1"→

Step 8

Now remove your plate from the mold. Draw a line across the center of your mold from side to side. (See Fig. 212.) This line on either side of the hollow will represent the middle spot between the bars of the handles. (See Fig. 213.) Place the handles on the circle with the line exactly in the middle between the bars. The rolled portion of the handle should be *1* inch from the hollow of the mold. Hold the curved handle flat on the top of the mold and hammer the ends into the shape of the hollow. (See Fig. 214.) Do the same to the handle on the opposite side. Lay the shaped plate into the hollow over the handle. The handles should be far enough out so that the rolled part of the handle is ½ inch from the edge of the plate. (See Fig. 215.) Move the bars of the handle nearer together or farther apart if necessary, but they seem best if they are attached so that the distance between them where

Fig. 214
Shaping handles on mold

Fig. 215
Fitting handle to Plate on mold

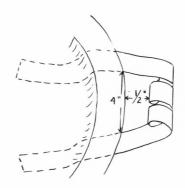

4" ←½"→

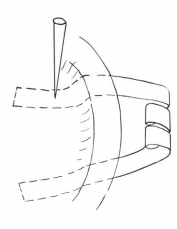

Fig. 216
Marking place for rivet
with scriber

Fig. 217
Marking Plate and handle
with center punch for rivet
placement

they meet the plate is 4 inches. (See Fig. 215.) Determine which of the ends of the circular design you prefer to be "up," and turn the plate in that position so that the handles are located to the left and right of it. Tap lightly to hold the plate down on the handle ends in the hollow of the mold. The rivet will later go through both the plate and the bar of the handle to fasten them together.

Step 9

Mark the point with your scriber ½ inch from the edge of the border, over the middle of the bar. (See Fig. 216.) Still holding handle and plate in the mold, place the center punch on your mark and tap smartly with a hammer to mark a dent in both plate and handle. (See Fig. 217.) Remove the plate and the marked handle from the mold. With ⅛-inch bit in your drill, place the plate on a piece of waste wood and drill a hole on the mark. Place the handle in the vise and drill through the marks. (See Fig. 218.) File off the burr on the under side of the cut.

Fig. 218
Piercing handle for rivet

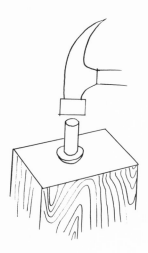

Fig. 219
Making a riveting set

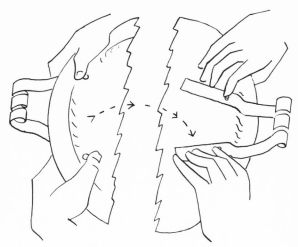

Fig. 220
Holding handle, Plate, and rivets securely together while turning Plate over for riveting

Step 10

A riveting set is very reasonable and is available at all handicraft supply stores. It includes a metal stake to fasten into your vise, with hollows to fit your rivet head. However, it is possible to work without a special riveting set, if you do this:

Fasten a small piece of hardwood upright in your vise (the piece used as a mold for the powder scoop will do). Set it with the end of the wood facing up, as it is in Fig. 221. Turn one of your rivets head down on the wood and hammer lightly twice on the other end of the rivet. (See Fig. 219.) This depression will be used in setting your rivets.

Set your rivet through the hole in the plate and the hole in the handle. Set the handle exactly in position and, holding them all firmly, turn the plate upside down (see Fig. 220) and place it with the rivet head on the hollow you have formed in the wooden block. Press the metal plate and handle strip together over the rivet so the rivet will extend as much as pos-

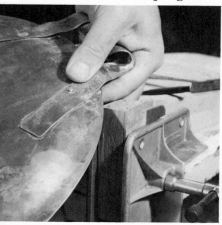

Fig. 221
Holding rivet through handle and Plate before placing on riveting set in vise

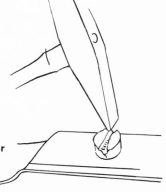

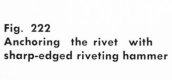

Fig. 222
Anchoring the rivet with sharp-edged riveting hammer

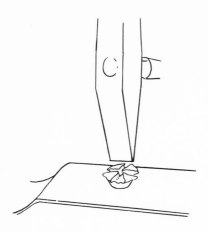

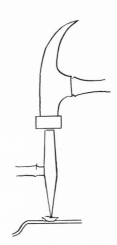

Fig. 223
Cross blow with riveting
hammer to tighten rivet
in place

Fig. 224
Double-hammer method of
further tightening

sible. (See Fig. 221.) The stem of the rivet will be too long. With your cutting pliers, cut off all but $\frac{1}{16}$ of an inch. The rivet stem should extend up from the copper handle no more than $\frac{1}{16}$ inch after cutting. Still holding the pieces and the rivet in place, take your riveting hammer and with the sharp end hit the rivet hard, cross-wise. (See Fig. 222.) Strike it again at right angles (Fig. 223) and once again, always with the sharp blade of the hammer hitting the rivet. This spreads it and anchors it in the hole, tightening the rivet in place. Hold the riveting hammer in place on the rivet, sharp edge down, and strike it sharply once or twice with another hammer. (See Fig. 224.) This will prevent marks on the copper around the rivet because of misplaced blows. Now, with the flat side of the riveting hammer strike several hard blows on the rivet to spread it further. (See Fig. 225.) Turn your piece around. You will find that the handle and plate are fastened together tightly with the rivet and that the copper head is decorative on the surface of the plate.

Fig. 225
Final spreading of rivet

After the first rivet is in place, replace the plate in the mold. Arrange the handle held by one rivet, so that the second can be marked. Tap with the center punch and proceed from there to set the second rivet. To attach the second handle, repeat the whole process used for the other handle. First set the handle in place on the mold exactly opposite the first handle already attached.

Use the middle line on the mold as a guide, and measure to be sure that the rolled part is ½ inch from the plate. With the rivets in place the handles should be firm, and the under parts closely pressed to the shape of the bottom of the plate.

Step 11

Polish well and oxidize with a fresh solution of liver of sulphur; then polish very well with steel wool.

This whole project can be done with a 12-inch ready-cut circle to produce a handsome smaller plate without a rim, using the same mold for shaping. (See Fig. 226.)

Fig. 226
12-inch rimless Plate using
same procedures

Part 3. 12-inch Square Plate

(See photo of finished plate on p. 124)

The square plate follows all etching processes of the round plate, but the finding of its design is an interesting example of how freedom to experiment can act as a release to the imagination. In this square plate the method used (referred to in Chapter 1) is excellent for trying out any design you think you would like. By cutting out various motifs, moving them about in new combinations, fresh and interesting designs can be developed. Remember; try anything and trust your judgment. Start out always with the design sheet cut to the basic shape of your project. In this case it is the square, with the corners rounded. The two motifs (see Fig. 227) were cut out, perhaps twenty-five of each, and moved about to form this design. (See Fig. 228.) They might have been arranged to form a border around the square, or a circle within it, or in separate motifs, but in each the feeling of the person arranging the scraps of paper is the measure of what results are to be attained. The feeling that anything can be accomplished at will is the most rewarding and productive result of this method. A design such as this made of separate units depends for much of its success also on a fairly deep etch. If you wish to use our design, you will find it reproduced in actual-size sections in Fig. 229.

You will notice that the corners of the plate are rounded much more than usual. Repeat this curved corner on your design sheet—it is important to the general effect. Bevel, trace, scribe, and paint your plate with asphaltum as usual, and follow etching instructions in Chapter 2. Etch this plate to fully ⅓ of the thickness of the copper.

For plates of this 12-inch size, the regulation pyrex containers are too small. Photographic supply stores will carry the larger size up to 16 or 20 inches. However, if you are willing to construct a rough but workable etching bin which will take care of the largest projects in this book (or several of the smaller ones at once), see the end of this chapter for a method of making such a bin.

Fig. 227
Source of design for Square Plate

Fig. 228
Planning design for Square Plate

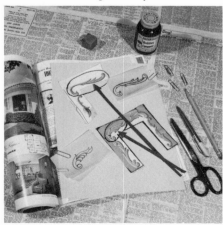

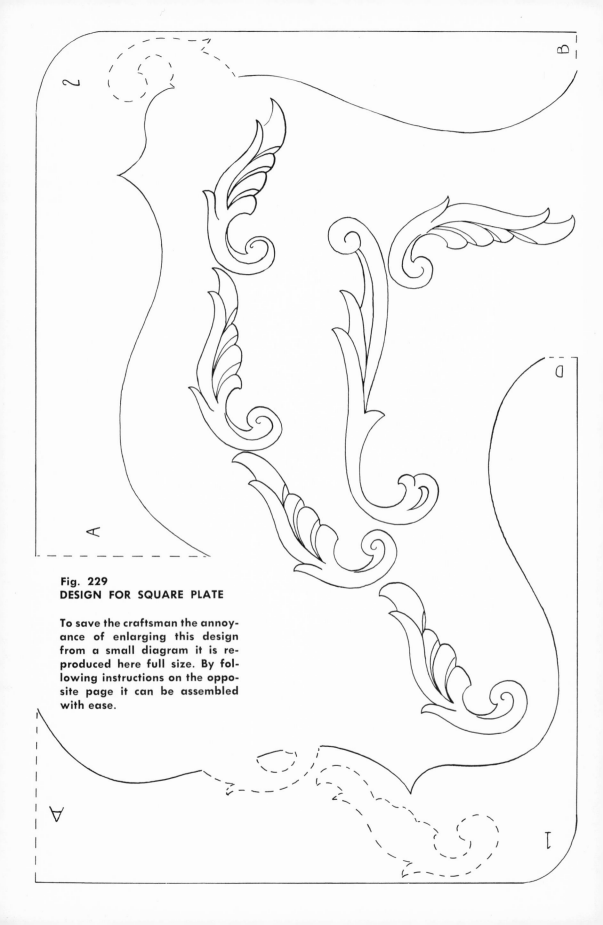

Fig. 229
DESIGN FOR SQUARE PLATE

To save the craftsman the annoyance of enlarging this design from a small diagram it is reproduced here full size. By following instructions on the opposite page it can be assembled with ease.

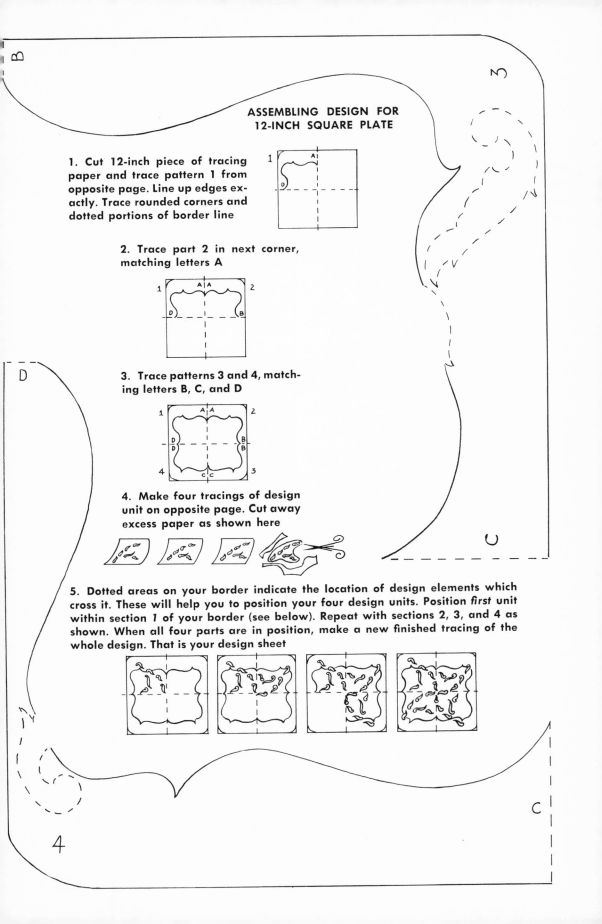

ASSEMBLING DESIGN FOR 12-INCH SQUARE PLATE

1. Cut 12-inch piece of tracing paper and trace pattern 1 from opposite page. Line up edges exactly. Trace rounded corners and dotted portions of border line

2. Trace part 2 in next corner, matching letters A

3. Trace patterns 3 and 4, matching letters B, C, and D

4. Make four tracings of design unit on opposite page. Cut away excess paper as shown here

5. Dotted areas on your border indicate the location of design elements which cross it. These will help you to position your four design units. Position *first* unit within section 1 of your border (see below). Repeat with sections 2, 3, and 4 as shown. When all four parts are in position, make a new finished tracing of the whole design. That is your design sheet

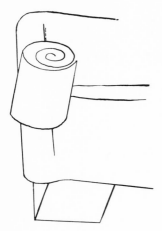

Fig. 230
Turning up edges of Square
Plate

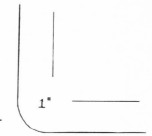

Fig. 231
Raise sides of Plate to within 1 inch of corners

When your square plate is etched, you will need:

1 piece of hardwood, preferably up to
11 inches long and about 3 inches wide

Set the wood on the table and set the plate face down upon it, extending the edge about ⅜ of an inch. Hold firmly and tap the edge of the copper plate over slightly at a 15° angle or thereabouts with the buckskin mallet. (See Fig. 230.) Do each of the four sides of the plate, but do not attempt to turn the corners. They will take part of the curve if you shape the edges down to 1 inch from each corner. (See Fig. 231.)

Polish, oxidize, and polish again.

Spray with lacquer if you wish on each of these plates, but be sure that your oxidizing and your polish are exactly as you want them before you lacquer your plates.

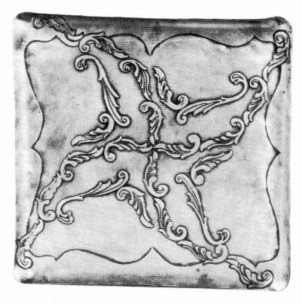

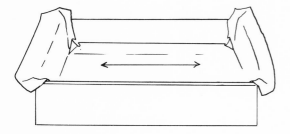

Fig. 232
Roofing paper across length
of box

HOW TO MAKE AN OUTSIZE ETCHING BIN

Get a wooden box, such as is used by vegetable dealers (solid, not slatted), at least 19 x 25 inches in size. Line this with tar roofing paper laid along one side, cut to 2 inches wider than the box and long enough to line it. Starting at the upper edge of one side (with 2 inches left higher than the edge), run the tar roofing paper down the side, across the bottom, and up again on the other side, with an extra 2 inches left above the edge; then cut off. (See Fig. 232.) Do the same in the opposite direction, laying the tar roofing paper cross-wise over the other on the bottom of the box. (See Fig. 233.)

Fig. 233
Roofing paper across *width*
of box

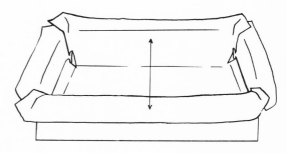

You will find that in the corners there will be an extra 1 inch on each side of the roofing paper. Lay it in as close to the box as possible, and lay the extra paper from the opposite direction as smoothly as possible over it. (See Fig. 234.) This makes a good protection for the corner. Press the paper in place against the inner corner of the box, but be careful not to crack the brittle roofing paper. Then turn the extra 2 inches of the roofing paper over the top of the box and nail it on the *outside* all around. (See Fig. 235.) Now melt paraffin and drop a thick layer closely along all inside edges of the roofing paper and at each corner to the very top. (See Fig. 236.)

While a box such as this seems a great deal of trouble to go to for one project, it is of repeated usefulness in allowing you to etch many projects together. Two 12-inch plates and many small projects can be done in a box of this size, thus assuring an identical depth of etch and a saving of acid. Besides, if it is rinsed well in cold water and dried after each use, the bin can be used indefinitely and stored anywhere between usings. Care should be exercised in keeping the wax replenished at need. Always test the box before each usage by pouring cold water into it to make sure the liquid does not leak out of the corners.

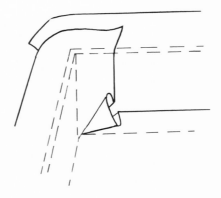

Fig. 234
Fitting roofing paper close to corner of box

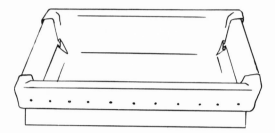

Fig. 235
Roofing paper nailed to
outside of box

Fig. 236
Protection of corners and
exposed edges with paraffin

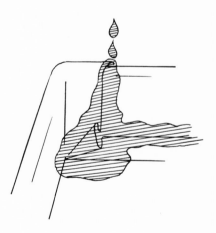

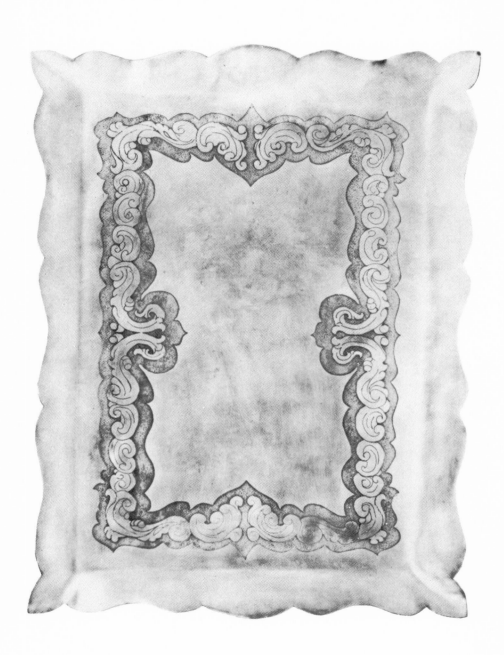

Chapter 12

A LARGE TEA TRAY IN COPPER

In addition to the materials on hand, you will need, to begin:

1 sheet of 18-gauge copper 17 x 23 inches
2 pieces of hardwood 1 x 3 x 12 inches
2 pieces of hardwood 1 x 3 x 19 inches (optional)
1 box of paraffin (3 or 4 squares)
1 roll of cellophane tape

First prepare your design carefully.

Note how this design was evolved from a printed border in a magazine advertisement. (See Fig. 237.) You may use the same method in finding another design for your tray, or use this.

In large projects such as this it is especially important to use the strong clear quality of tracing paper used by architects. If you buy this paper in a roll, your design sheet will not have to be pieced.

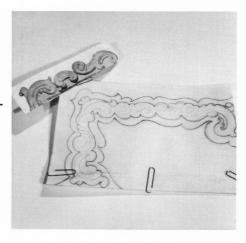

Fig. 237
**Design evolved from print-
ed border in a magazine**

Fig. 238
Design of large Tea Tray—
exact size

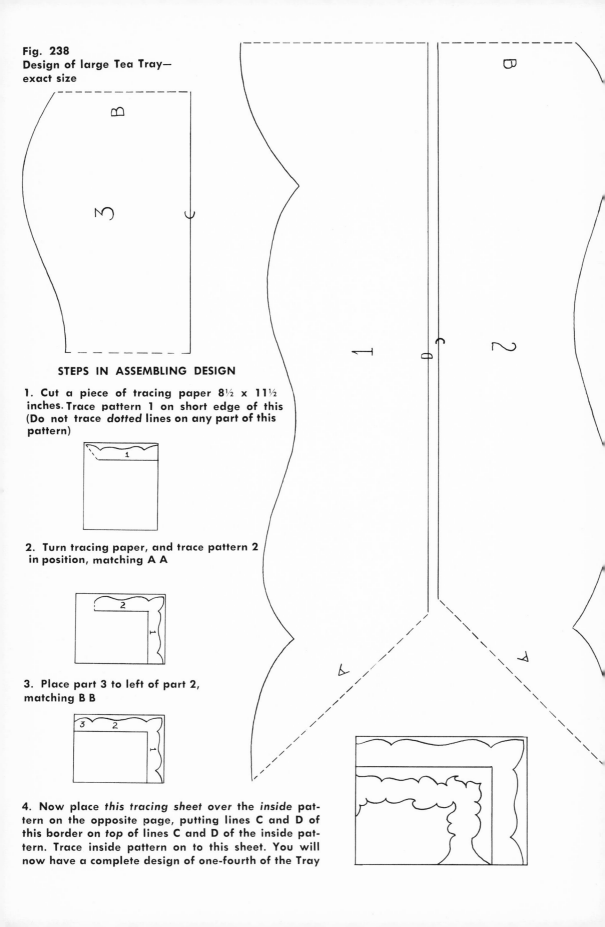

STEPS IN ASSEMBLING DESIGN

1. Cut a piece of tracing paper 8½ x 11½ inches. Trace pattern 1 on short edge of this (Do not trace *dotted* lines on any part of this pattern)

2. Turn tracing paper, and trace pattern 2 in position, matching A A

3. Place part 3 to left of part 2, matching B B

4. Now place *this tracing sheet* over the *inside* pattern on the opposite page, putting lines C and D of this border on *top* of lines C and D of the inside pattern. Trace inside pattern on to this sheet. You will now have a complete design of one-fourth of the Tray

5. Take your fresh piece of tracing paper, 17 x 23 inches, and trace the complete quarter pattern four times in the positions shown above. E is traced as is. F is reversed and traced from the *back* of the sheet. G is just turned upside down. H is both reversed and turned upside down.

Step 1

Cut two sheets to the size of the copper, 17 x 23 inches. If you find it in a pad, you may have to join two or more pieces to cover the entire surface. In such a case, overlap the edges no more than ¼ inch and paste the parts together with rubber cement. When you trace your design, mark it very carefully over these seams.

If this design is to be used on your tray, trace the design which is presented in Fig. 238, after it has been assembled according to instructions that are given with the design.

Use one of the two sheets of tracing paper (17 x 23 inches) to trace the full design of the tray, including the scallops and the ruled rectangle from Fig. 238.

On the second full size sheet, trace only the scalloped edge and the ruled rectangle.

You now have two design sheets—one with the full design, and one with only the scalloped edge and the ruled rectangle.

Step 2

Choose the better side of your sheet of copper. (One side of the copper you buy in sheets is generally freer of blemishes than the other.) Clean and paint it white as usual, and trace and scribe on it the design of your tray. Trace also the ruled rectangle—use a ruler—but do not mark the scallops. Wash off the white tempera and dry the tray well. Turn your copper over. Lay over it the scallop sheet and line up the edges of the paper and the copper, after slipping carbon paper under the lines of the rectangle. Rule on this, the back of the tray, *only* the lines of the rectangle—nothing else. (See Fig. 239.) This is to help with the later turning up of the edges of the tray. By pressing hard on the pencil when you trace the lines, you will get enough carbon on the copper to be able to scribe this one rectangle without first painting the tray-back with tempera. Scribe this line in the back just as you do the others on the right side of your tray.

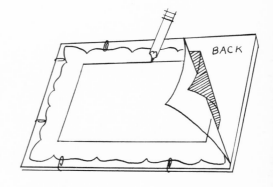

Fig. 239
Pattern sheet with only scallops and guiding line for shaping is clipped to back of Tray to mark rectangle for scribing

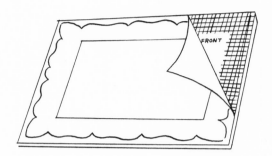

Fig. 240
Same pattern sheet is now pasted on *right* side of Tray (with rubber cement applied 2 inches deep from edge) as guide to cutting scallops

FRONT

Now paste this same tracing sheet with the scallops and the lined rectangle only, on the right side of your tray, lining up the copper and paper edges carefully. Make sure that the rubber cement is spread fully 2 inches in from the edge. (See Fig. 240.) Cut the scallops out, following the line on the paper. Make sure that the paper is firmly fastened in place during the cutting.

Step 3

You are now ready to cut the scalloped edges on your copper. If you are a man, you will probably be strong enough to cut part of this scalloped edge with the tinsnips. Women generally must use the jeweler's saw for the whole procedure. In that case the 8-inch jeweler's saw is recommended because it gives leeway for movement in every direction. (The use of this saw is discussed in Chapter 5.)

Bevel and smooth all edges, and blunt the sharp points at the corners of your tray by filing them slightly round.

You have now a completely scribed tray with the scallops cut out and beveled smoothly and the ruled line of the rectangle scribed on both front and back. You are now ready to raise the sides of your tray, before you paint with asphaltum.

By turning up the edges at this point, you make it unnecessary to paint the back with asphaltum, since the tray itself becomes the etching container. It will be slightly more awkward to paint the design with asphaltum than if the tray were flat, but it is large enough not to be too difficult.

Fig. 241
Lining up boards above and below copper in position to attach C clamps

Step 4. Turning Up the Tray

Place one of the 12-inch boards along the straight scribed line at one end of your tray. Place the other board on the other side of the copper directly under the first board, sandwiching the copper between them. (See Fig. 241.) Place your C clamps as they appear in Fig. 241, so that they hold the sides of the boards firmly in place. Before finally tightening your clamps, see that each board touches the lines exactly for its entire length. Once the boards are firmly clamped in the proper place, turn the tray upside down and place (overhanging by 3 inches) on a firm, solid ledge or table. (See Fig. 242.) Be sure your table is well padded with thick newspaper. With a buckskin mallet, tap the metal beyond the wood, being careful to use the flat face of the mallet to avoid marks on the metal. Do not hit too hard, and work not from the corner but from where the wood begins. Continue across to the other end of the wood. The final angle we wish to achieve is approximately 30° from the horizontal. Tap gradually with overlapping strokes, taking several trips back and forth to achieve the proper angle with a smooth bend. By taking it slowly we can correct as we go along any irregularities from uneven tapping. Repeat at the opposite end. The same wood can be used for the same method on the long side, but it must be done in two operations of clamping. However, if you use for the long side two 19-inch lengths of board, it will be simpler. (See Fig. 243.)

Fig. 242
Shaping end of Tray

Fig. 243
Shaping side of Tray

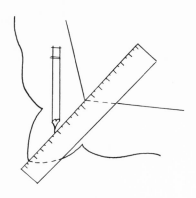

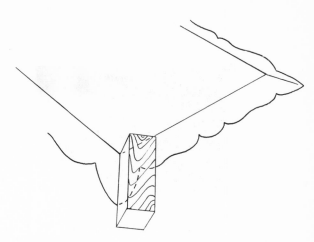

Fig. 244
Penciling line across exact corner

Fig. 245
Position of wood for shaping corner

This still leaves the corners irregular and not sufficiently raised. With a pencil and a ruler, draw a line from the fold you find underneath each corner of your tray to the point of that same corner. (See Fig. 244.) Lay the end of one of your 12 inches of wood against one of the narrow ends of your tray so that its corner touches the point of the corner fold and its edge runs along your penciled line to the pointed edge of the tray. (See Fig. 245.) Set your second board exactly underneath the copper to match, and clamp, away from the side to be hammered, as shown in Fig. 245. By tightening your clamp accurately and firmly in place, you will find you have raised the side of the corner exactly enough. Hammer the opposite side of the same corner to the same angle (see Fig. 246) and remove your clamp. Repeat at each corner, clamping the wood on the end (short) sides, not the long, on all four corners. Your tray should now be raised so that all four sides are at the same angle, and all four corners are at the lower angle, but identical with each other.

Fig. 246
Shaping corner with buck-skin mallet

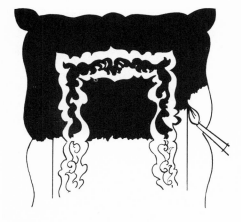

Fig. 247
Tray painted with asphaltum

Step 5

You are now ready to paint with asphaltum.

Before you begin to paint the design in asphaltum, consider how you will manage. With so large a surface, it is better to work on one section at a time, keeping the other parts covered. We suggest a quarter because it is a workable size, and in a flowing design such as this it is helpful to see several units at once.

By this time the tray has been handled and exposed to the air so that it will need cleaning again. Clean the whole surface and cover all but the quarter you will be working on with a clean cloth or a large piece of clean paper, and proceed to paint the design in asphaltum. Then paint up to the scalloped edges of your plate, and on the large flat center that is clear of design. (See Fig. 247.) It is always helpful to keep your design sheet before you for reference as you paint your project.

When your entire tray is painted and you are ready to etch, you will find the corners are not as high as the sides and therefore will not allow your etching bath the depth it requires. (See Fig. 248.) To alleviate this and to permit you to make as deep an etch as you wish in the tray, follow the instructions below for making a protective wall of paraffin in each corner.

Fig. 248
Lowered angle of corner—
reason for paraffin pocket

Fig. 249
Cellophane tape for wall of
pocket

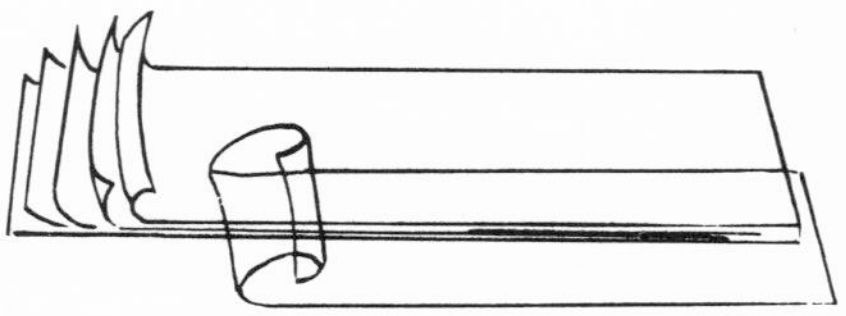

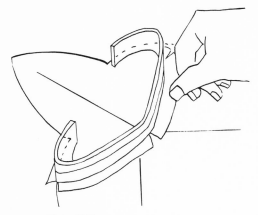

Fig. 250
Attaching front wall of
cellophane for pocket

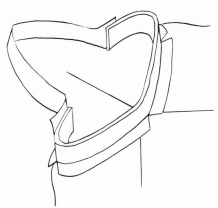

Fig. 251
Completing construction of
pocket

Step 6

Cut five pieces of 1-inch cellophane tape each 7 inches long and lay one over the other to make a thick piece of cellophane 1 x 7 inches. Cut another strip 7 inches long. Lay this along the thick cellophane strip, attached firmly by ½ its width. (See Fig. 249.) This you will use as a cellophane wall across each corner of the tray, leaving one sticky surface exposed. Fasten this upright at 3½ inches from each corner of your tray, attaching one end firmly to the asphalted metal. It should reach at each edge to about 3½ inches from the corner. (See Fig. 250.) Be sure this strip is attached down into the hollow of the corner. Rub your thumb over the attached edge to seal it firmly. Then take one single 7-inch strip of the tape and attach it to one edge of this wall and continue round the corner of the tray till it reaches the other edge of the thick tape wall. (See Fig. 251.) This strip should also be upright, with the long edge of the strip firmly fastened to the outer edge of the tray. (See Fig. 252.) You have now constructed a triangular pocket which must be leak-proof. To test this, slowly pour three teaspoons of cold water into the pockets you have constructed. If any water leaks out under the tape, repair it at that point with more tape.

Fig. 252
Detail of underside attaching

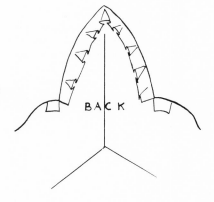

BACK

Step 7

When the pocket is leak-proof, slowly pour, preferably by spoonfuls, the melted paraffin. (See Fig. 253.) Let the paraffin cool for a second after removing it from the fire, but you will have to remelt it often to fill all four corners.

If the wax should run out, stop the leak at once, and scrape off any wax from the exposed copper; the part of the design it covers will not be etched —the wax acts like asphaltum on those spots. Leave the paraffin overnight to harden. In the morning, take off the thick strips of Scotch Tape nearest the design. (See Fig. 254.) You now have a wall ¾ inch high in each corner to help keep your acid in the tray. Etch as usual in copper mordant or nitric acid 3 to 1. (See Chapter 2.) Remember, if you are using the nitric acid solution, measure and pour the *water* into the tray *first*. Then pour in the nitric acid as in Chapter 2.

It will be a little more difficult to determine the depth of the etch than when you are using a separate container from which you can remove your piece, rinse it, and examine it. In this you must depend on gently sliding the wooden clothespin along part of the design exposed to the acid to the edges covered by the asphaltum, to feel the depth of the ridge. If you find that a pointed strip of scrap copper instead of the clothespin would make it easier for you to judge, use that.

This method works for the large tray, because the turning up of the edges and the paraffining of the corners makes it possible to use it as its own container. For large pieces such as this, you can construct your own bin and paint and etch the piece flat before turning it up. That would save you the trouble of constructing the paraffined corners, but you would have to paint the back of the tray with asphaltum. One satisfaction of the large bin (described in Chapter 11) is that you can plan to etch several pieces together, thus ensuring an even etch and a saving of acid. Sometimes there is no choice; in this case there is, as the sides are raised. With this tray, we chose to raise them first and etch the design in the tray itself. We have often etched trays like it flat in a large etching bin with equal success. You are the one to weigh the differences and make the decision.

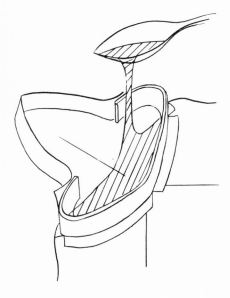

Fig. 253
Filling cellophane frame with paraffin

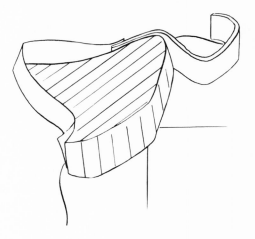

Fig. 254
Removing cellophane to expose protective triangle of paraffin on corner of Tray to be etched

Steps 8–10

When your tray is etched—by whichever method—clean the asphaltum off as usual with turpentine and wipe it dry.

You are now ready to stipple the background of your design. Follow the directions in Chapter 11 on stippling.

After the background is completely stippled, clean your tray well with steel wool and oxidize with fresh liver of sulphur. Highlight the design areas and the large clear areas on your tray. Leave enough of the oxidizing in the design background to give character to the general effect. When you are sure of the effect you have achieved, lacquer your tray, following closely instructions on the can.

Chapter 13

A SERVING CENTERPIECE

THIS PROJECT CARRIES WITHIN IT MANY OF THE SKILLS ACQUIRED IN THOSE that precede it. But the riveting in the handled copper plate in Chapter 10 was fairly simple. In this centerpiece, the riveting calls for great precision. There are handmade hinges here that are difficult to make, and this is the first project in the book that calls for such hinges. You will need to practice well on scrap copper.

Yet this is a handsome and rewarding piece to make. If you feel that you are willing to tackle it, you will find exact measurements and explicit directions to help you. If you are a person who works with precision, you will enjoy doing it and will do it well. You will, nevertheless, find it a challenge.

This project consists of a frame into which copper plates, made previously and now in use, can be slipped when needed. It uses as its cover the 13-inch handled plate presented in Chapter 11 (see Fig. 255) and has two identical shelves, of which one is the 12-inch plate shown in the same chapter. (See Fig. 256).

Its inspiration came from an ancient ceremonial piece in a museum, but its possibilities as a modern aid to entertaining are endless. With fruit arranged on top, sandwiches or decorative salads and cake on the inside trays (that slide out all ready for serving), this makes a handsome and practical aid to a tea, bridge, or buffet supper.

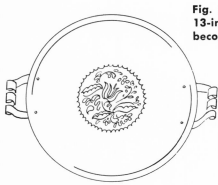

Fig. 255
13-inch tray (Chapter 11)
becomes cover of Centerpiece

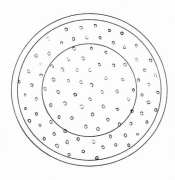

Fig. 256
Two   identical   12-inch
plates (Chapter 11) become
shelves of Centerpiece

In addition to the materials on hand, you will need, to begin:

2 pieces of 18-gauge copper, each 7¼ inches x 19⅞ inches
2 pieces of 16-gauge copper, each ½ inch x 19 inches
2 pieces of 16-gauge copper, each ½ inch x 23 inches
3 pieces of 18-gauge copper, each ½ inch x 12¼ inches
4 pieces of 16-gauge copper, each ½ inch x 6⅜ inches
1 piece of 18-gauge copper, ½ inch x 2⅛ inches
1 12-inch circle of 18-gauge copper for the base
4 ft. copper wire, Browne & Sharpe, 14-gauge
¼ lb. ⅛ x ¼ inch long copper rivets
1 high-speed twist drill—⅛-inch

Estimate from the above measurements the amount of copper you will need. It must be bought in a sheet or sheets to be cut at home with tinsnips.

When you are ready to work, mark out on your copper the large rectangles (7¼ x 19⅞ inches), the strips, and the 12-inch circle. Cut these out.

In cutting the strips—this is very important—go slowly! Mark them all but do not cut them without resting between strips. Tired hands send you off the line. As you cut the strips, they curl up; straighten them by hand after cutting as much as possible; then flatten with a buckskin mallet on one long piece of wood if possible. You will find that there is a slight arc when the strips are stood on end along the wood. (See Fig. 257.) This is because the metal is stretched by the cutting. Set your metal edgewise on your board. Starting at one end, hammer firmly with your buckskin mallet all along the edge. (See Fig. 258.) Check for gaps between the metal and the wood and tap further if necessary. Then turn the copper over to the opposite edge and check there. Tap along this edge also to assure straight edges. Then tap lightly on the flat surface to make sure of no change there. Lay these aside temporarily.

Fig. 257
Copper strips often stretch in the cutting

Fig. 258
Correcting the arc caused by stretching

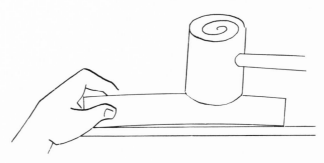

142

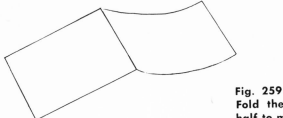

Fig. 259
Fold the design sheet in
half to mark center line

The Centerpiece Walls

One of the two large rectangular pieces (7¼ x 19⅝ inches) forms the back of the centerpiece; the other the front. One rectangle will later be cut in half to make the doors. Both of these long pieces will be etched, so you must now prepare your design sheet.

Cut one piece of tracing paper to the exact size of one of your rectangles (7¼ x 19⅝ inches). The same design will repeat on both front and back, so this design sheet is all you will need. Fold your paper in half so as to give two rectangles 7¼ x 9¹⁵⁄₁₆ inches. (See Fig. 259.) Draw a line along the crease to mark the middle. Draw two lines parallel to your center line, ⁹⁄₁₆ inch on each side, and a line along each short end, ⅜ inch from the edge. (See Fig. 260.)

Fig. 260
Lines measured to mark
placement of design units
and of the hinges

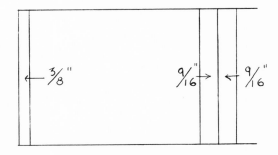

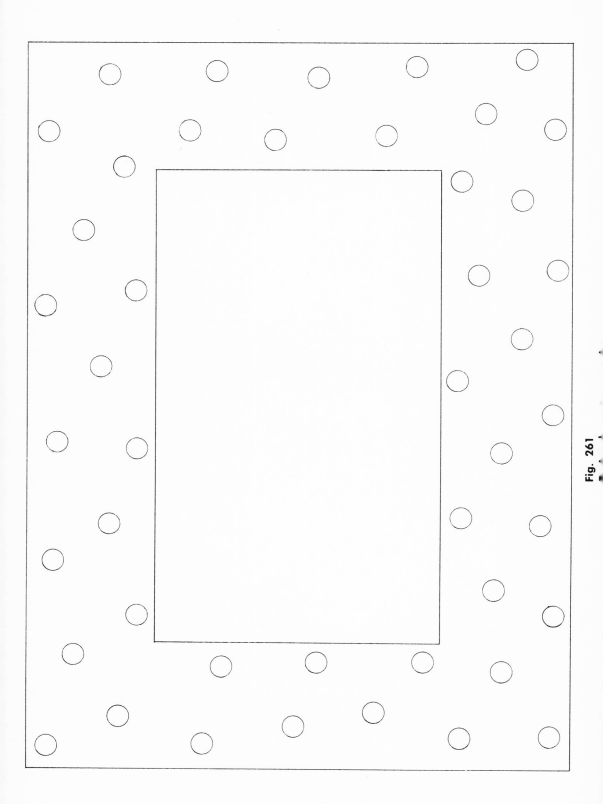

Fig. 261

144

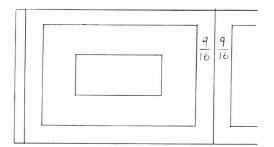

Fig. 262
Placement of design unit

You are now ready to prepare the design itself. Trace with a ruler two copies of the design for this centerpiece given in Fig. 261, and trace in the crescents for all the dots. Now take your long folded sheet and place one of these traced designs on each side of the crease—setting them against the lines you have already drawn $\frac{9}{16}$ inch to either side of the center. Place them at an even distance from top and bottom. (See Fig. 262.) Paste them in place with rubber cement.

You now have your design sheet ready. You can, therefore, go on to clean your copper rectangles. Paint them in tempera, trace and scribe your design on each, ready for painting with asphaltum. Remember, scribe the lines with a ruler, and to indicate placement of the dots, scribe only a crescent. (See Fig. 263.)

Paint the back and turn over on double newsprint as usual.

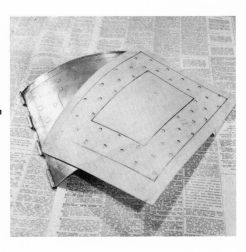

Fig. 263
Design sheet and design etched on copper door

First, paint the small rectangle solidly with asphaltum; then paint the dots, using the drop method shown in Chapter 11. Last, paint from the outer rectangles clear to all edges, covering the lines scribed ⅜ inch from the short ends. These are marks placed for the hinges; they are not to be used in relation to painting with asphaltum. Also paint the strip in the middle of each copper piece between the two large rectangles. (See Fig. 264.) After you have completed etching and the asphaltum is cleaned off with turpentine, note your scribed lines ⅜ inch from each end of the two sheets of copper. Before you go any further, choose the better piece for the front of your centerpiece, depending on the quality of your etch and any scratches which may mar your copper.

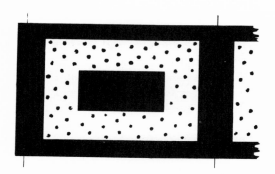

Fig. 264
Asphaltum protects all areas not to be etched

Making the Hinges

The front piece will have four hinges at each end and the back piece only three. (See front piece shown in Fig. 263.) On your scribed lines on both ends of both pieces ⅜ inch from the edge, measure down 1⅛ inch. Mark lightly with your scriber. (Fig. 265.) Do the same thing on the corresponding edge of the copper. Draw a line with your scriber to connect the marks. (See Fig. 265.) Repeat the procedure from the bottom with the same 1⅛-inch measurement, as shown in Fig. 265. Again from the top measure down, this time 2⅛ inches from the top edge. Repeat the entire procedure as used for the 1⅛-inch measurement. When this is completed, do the same for 3⅛ inches, 4⅛ inches, and 5⅛ inches, all measured from the top edge. You now have scribed lines for a top and bottom hinge of 1⅛ inches and five hinges of 1 inch each. (See Fig. 266.)

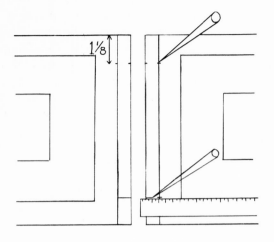

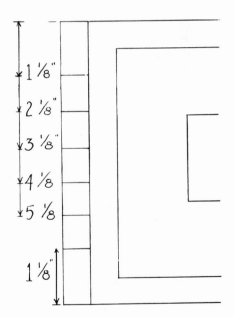

Fig. 265
Measuring and scribing
guide lines for hinges

Fig. 266
Hinge lines measured and
scribed

To make sure that you remove the metal from the proper areas, take the sheet that is to be your front piece. Counting from the top with your scriber, mark an X on every *second* section. (See Fig. 267.) Those marked with X's are to be *cut out*. Mark the X's at both the left and right ends of the *front* sheet. On your back sheet place an X on the 1st, 3rd, 5th, and 7th sections of both ends. (See Fig. 268.) With your jeweler's saw cut out all the parts marked with an X on both ends of both pieces. If your cutting has been accurate, your two pieces (back and front) should interlock. (See Fig. 269.) If they do not quite fit, do not file now. It will be easier after the hinges are turned.

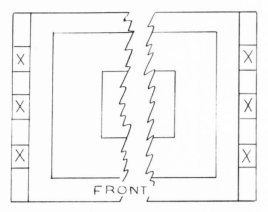

Fig. 267
X marks areas to be cut out
on *front* hinges

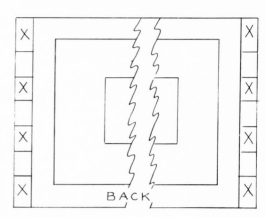

Fig. 268
X marks areas to be cut out
on *back* hinges

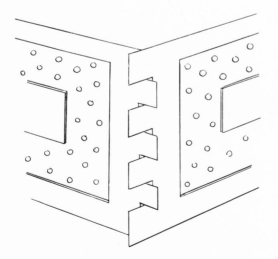

Fig. 269
Testing interlocking of hinges

Fig. 270
Marking guide lines for
first step in turning hinges

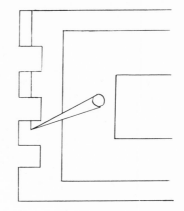

Measure in $\frac{3}{16}$ of an inch from the outside edge of each hinge and scribe a line on the etched side down all hinges, crossing these marks. (See Fig. 270.) Do this on both ends of each sheet.

You will now need:

a few nails (only slightly larger in diameter than the copper wire for the hinge)

2 strips of hardwood (your block from the powder scoop will do for one of these)

metal ruler (such as is found in a combination square)

Clamp your blocks of wood in front and back of your front sheet of copper, leaving the hinges showing and the top edges of the wood just touching the *scribed* line, $\frac{3}{16}$ from the edge. (See Fig. 271.) Place whole unit in your vise, as it appears in Fig. 273. Now lay a nail on the front wood block against the first hinge to be shaped. Hold it in place against the copper with the end edge of the metal ruler. (See Fig. 272.) One caution: on all but the top

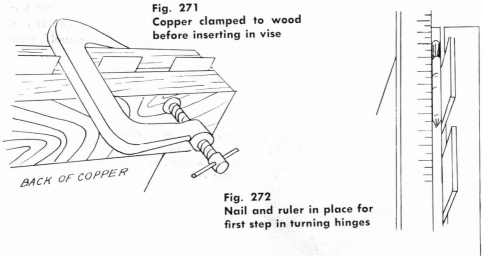

Fig. 271
Copper clamped to wood
before inserting in vise

BACK OF COPPER

Fig. 272
Nail and ruler in place for
first step in turning hinges

Fig. 273
Bending first 3/16 inch of
hinge over nail

Fig. 275
Shaping hinge with ruler
removed

and bottom hinges it may be necessary to cut the head off the nail before
using it in order to remove the nail easily when the hinge is completed.

With a buckskin mallet, tap the copper from the back until it touches the
ruler in front. (See Fig. 273.) Check from time to time to make sure that
the copper has not slipped, that the wood is still touching the scribed line.

Next loosen the vise and clamp and move the blocks down so that they
are just touching the first mark—⅜ inch from the edge, and tap again until
the hinge touches the ruler. (See Fig. 274.) *Note*: this project has been temporarily turned around in the vise in order to show in the photo the other
side of the curve and edge of the hinge.

Remove the ruler and tap the hinge further until it touches the wood
block. (See Fig. 275.) The first curve of each hinge is most important. If
it is not sufficiently rounded, the hole will be oval-shaped and may not line
up with the other hinges. Remove your metal from the vise. Take any of
your larger hardwood molds and lay your sheet of metal on the mold, with

Fig. 274
Shaping the total 3/8 inch
of hinge over nail (project
turned around in vise for
better view)

Fig. 276
Rounding hinge further,
against ruler back in position

the curve of the hinge up and the nail still caught within it. Again place the
ruler against the nail and with the buckskin mallet, tap again until the hinge
touches the ruler. (See Fig. 276.) Remove the ruler and with the nail still
in place hold the sheet of copper vertical with the hinge resting flat on the
mold as it is in Fig. 277. Tap the hinge as close to the main sheet of copper
as possible. Because of the round edges of the mallet it will not be possible
to turn the hinge far enough to secure the wire; so for this step you will use
your riveting hammer. First, slide a sheet of cardboard along the surface
of the copper sheet until it slips into the opening left under the hinge. (See
Fig. 277.) With the broad end of your riveting hammer, tap lightly until
the opening left between hinge and copper sheet is smaller than the diameter
of the copper wire you will use in the hinge. The cardboard is to prevent the
hammer from marking the copper. With a pair of pliers, remove the nail.
Repeat for all hinges. Remember always to curl your hinges toward the
etched side of your copper.

Fig. 277
Standing copper sheet on
end, with hinge at bottom,
to complete closing of hinge

After all hinges have been turned, try fitting them together. (See Fig. 278.) If they do not fit, place the two sheets of copper together and mark with a scriber where the overlap occurs. File down the obstructions with a flat file or the flat side of your half-round file. (See Fig. 279.) Check your fit frequently, as excessive filing will cause gaps and spoil the smooth look of your hinge.

Before testing your hinge with wire, it is necessary to curve the two sheets of copper so that both ends may be hinged at once. It is not necessary at this time to get a perfect circle. Any of your circular molds with an outside diameter anywhere from 6 to 10 inches will serve your present purpose.

Place your mold flat on the table. Place your sheet of copper along the edge and press the copper around by hand. (See Fig. 280.) Do this with both copper rectangles. Your ends will not be as curved as the center of your sheet, but this will be corrected later in the final shaping.

Cut off a test piece of wire to 12 inches long and push it through all hinges. (See Fig. 281.) It will be necessary to twist the wire as you push it through. Do not worry about bends or irregularities in your wire. As it is pushed through, it straightens out with just the pressure and the turning. *Caution*: as you push it, it may bend just at the point of entry to the top hinge. Straighten the wire by hand and push again until it goes through. You can follow the progress of the wire by checking individual hinges on one side or another by seeing which slots are closed, as in Fig. 281.

You are now ready to prepare your copper strips before assembling the serving centerpiece.

Two of the strips are ½ inch wide and 19 inches long. Two are ½ inch x 23 inches and three are ½ x 12¼ inches. Bevel and smooth edges of all of your half-inch-wide strips.

Preparing Shelf Clips

Take the three lengths of 12¼ inches, which are to be the supports for your shelves. Note carefully that all measurements you are going to make on these three strips must match exactly. With scriber and ruler make the following measurements:

Beginning from one end of each of these three strips, measure on each long edge and mark the following: ½ inch, 1 inch, 1½ inch, 3⅝ inch, 4⅛ inch, 4⅝ inch, 5⅛ inch, 5⅝ inch, 7¾ inch, 8¼ inch, 8¾ inch, 9¼ inch, 9¾ inch. All measurements are taken from one end of the strip.

You are now ready to bend your marked strips; but before bending, check all measurements again and make sure that all three strips line up in *all measurements*.

Fig. 278
Testing fit of hinge

Fig. 279
Filing top and bottom of
hinges where necessary, for
better fit

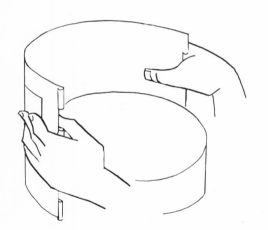

Fig. 280
Curving copper rectangles
by hand around smaller
mold

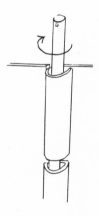

Fig. 281
Checking hinges by inserting wire

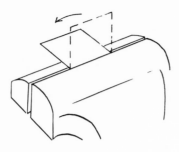

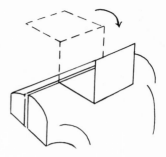

Fig. 282
Bending first ½ inch in vise

Fig. 283
Second bend in vise

Bending the Strips

Step 1

Place strip in vise with the first ½-inch mark just showing above and parallel to your vise, with the ½-inch end of the copper strip protruding. With your buckskin mallet, tap the end forward and down to a 90° right angle. (See Fig. 282.)

Step 2

Move the piece ½ inch in the vise to the next mark and tap the copper strip back in the other direction so as to make a step. (See Fig. 283.) Raise again to the next mark and bend in the same direction as in Step 1. Your strip should now appear as in Fig. 284.

Fig. 284
First three folds in strip completed

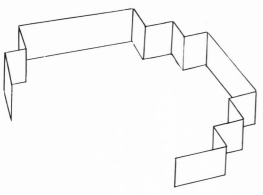

Fig. 285
Appearance of bent shelf
clips before sections are
pressed together

Fig. 286
Pressing sections of shelf
clips together

Now move to the 3⅝ inch line, follow Step 1 above, move another ½ inch and follow Step 2, another ½ inch and follow Step 1 again, the next ½ inch follows Step 2, and the one following is Step 1 again. Move down the strip to the next set of folds and follow exactly the previous five folds.

What you have now is a strip of copper bent as in Fig. 285. Press each section together by hand like an accordion. With your long-nosed pliers, press together each section firmly, as shown in Fig. 286. These are the clips to hold the 12-inch plates which form the shelves of the serving centerpiece. Turn your strip clips down on a small block of hardwood. With your buckskin mallet, flatten the straight areas between the clips and at the ends. (See Fig. 287.) Place the strips flat so that the clips just hang over the edge and can be reset to the 90° angle to which they were originally bent.

Repeat complete bending procedure on the two remaining strips, and check again to make sure that all three sets of clips are on the same levels.

Fig. 287
Flattening the strip be-
tween clip sections

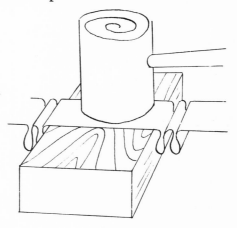

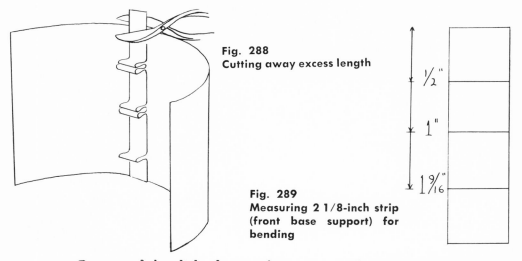

Fig. 288
Cutting away excess length

$\frac{1}{2}$"

1"

$1\frac{9}{16}$"

Fig. 289
Measuring 2 1/8-inch strip (front base support) for bending

Because of the slight degree of variation in the tightness of the folds, place the strips upright on the walls of the cabinet in their proper position. (See Figs. 299, 306.) The single fold must be ½ inch above the bottom. With your strip in this position, note whether the top of the strip juts above the upper ridge of the copper frame. Mark the point at which it meets the top of the centerpiece. (See Fig. 288.) Do this with each of the three pieces, cut off the excess, and file off the sharp edges.

Front Support for Base

With your ruler and scriber, mark the strip of copper, ½ x 2⅛ inches, as follows:

The first line scribed, again, should be ½ inch from one end; the next line will be 1 inch from the same end; the third line will be 1⁹⁄₁₆ inches, also from the same end. (See Fig. 289.) Place this strip in your vise, with the scribed line just showing above the vise jaw. As in previous strips, fold once, move the strip up and make the second fold in the opposite direction. The third fold differs. It should be in the same direction as the fold just before it, so that it will appear as in Fig. 290. Press together by hand (see Fig. 291) and complete the fold with the pliers so that the final result is as in Fig. 292. This is the bottom edge for the front of the centerpiece. The open ends will be riveted downward in the final assembling.

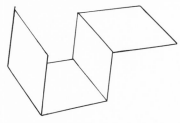

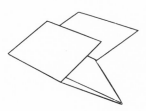

Fig. 290
Bending base support—Step 1

Fig. 291
Bending base support—Step 2

Fig. 292
Bending base support—Step 3

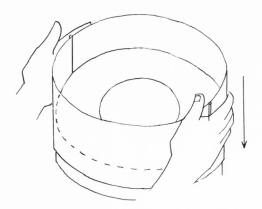

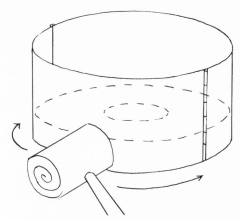

Fig. 293
Pressing the Centerpiece
frame into shape over mold

Fig. 294
Tapping lightly with buckskin mallet to shape closer
to mold

Shaping before Assembling

Before assembling the centerpiece, it would be wise to bring the piece as close to a perfect circle as you can. This final shaping would be more diffi-cult once the shelf clips were riveted in place.

Place the centerpiece over the 12-inch mold as in Fig. 293. You may have to force it on by pressing on the hinged portions to make it round. With the buckskin mallet, tap firmly from the center back sheet of copper out to the hinge. Be careful to tap on the copper only where it is supported by the mold inside. (See Fig. 294.) As you get closer to the hinge, tap a little harder, but be sure to keep your mallet flat so that you don't mar the copper. Work from the center to the other hinge and then repeat for the other sheet of copper. Turn your centerpiece upside down and slide the mold down so that you can tap the upper half of the centerpiece. Make sure the top of the centerpiece and the mold are both flush on the table before repeating the same hammering process given above.

Remove the mold and press in on the hinged sides very hard to accentuate the curves at the front and back of the centerpiece. (See Fig. 295.)

Fig. 295
Accentuating curve by
pressing hinged sides
toward each other

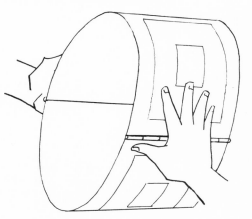

Assembling the Serving Centerpiece by Riveting

1. The Back Inner Frame

First, remove the temporary wires from your hinges.

On the back sheet of copper, there is a line scribed down the center. Measure ¼ inch from the top of this sheet down this line. Do the same from the bottom. Mark each point with your scriber. Now set this portion of your copper over a firm surface—your 12-inch mold set on edge will do for this. (See Fig. 296.)

With your center punch and a hammer, firmly mark these points *exactly* where the ¼-inch mark crosses the scribed center line. These marks are for the first rivet holes, and we use the center punch to ensure that the drill will not slip in making the holes. With your ⅛-inch drill bit in your hand drill, hold the copper in the same position on the edge of the mold and drill these holes. *Note:* it is important that your drill be perpendicular to your copper at this point so that the rivet will not slant in going through the hole.

Take both of the 19-inch strips and find the center point 9½ inches from either end. In the exact center from each end and from the sides, mark with the scriber. (See Fig. 297.) Place one strip against the top edge of your back copper sheet, bend it to the curve, the marked point against the larger piece. (See Fig. 298.) See that dot is centered in the hole. If so, center punch and drill this strip.

At the bottom of the middle of your back copper sheet, set the other 19-inch strip, and repeat. Always file off the burr left by the drill. Lay aside this strip for the moment.

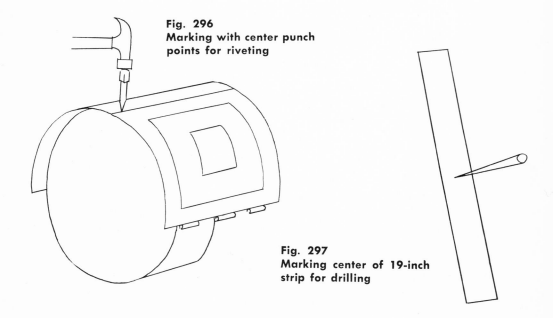

Fig. 296
Marking with center punch
points for riveting

Fig. 297
Marking center of 19-inch
strip for drilling

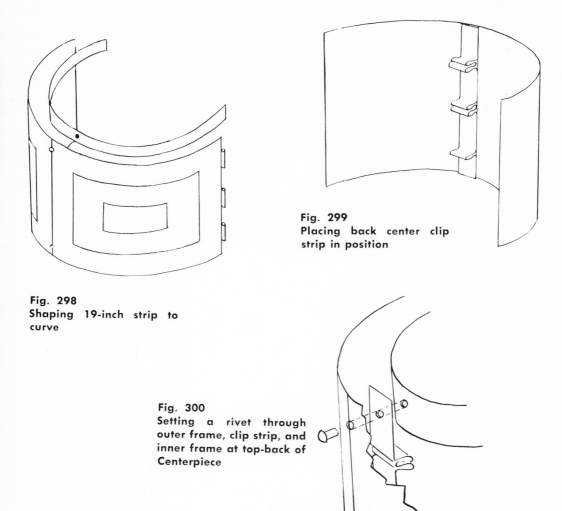

Fig. 298
Shaping 19-inch strip to curve

Fig. 299
Placing back center clip strip in position

Fig. 300
Setting a rivet through outer frame, clip strip, and inner frame at top-back of Centerpiece

2. The Shelf Strips

Decide which of your folded clip strips you are using for the middle of the back piece. Place this strip upright with the single fold at the bottom. (See Fig. 299.) With two C clamps, secure this strip in place so that the center of the strip is aligned with the outside line as shown through the holes top and bottom. (See Fig. 300.) With the folded strip firmly clamped in the exact position, scribe a circle through the holes onto the strip. Unclamp the strips and scribe the exact center of the circle you scribed through the hole. Center-punch and drill. This strip should be held in the vise or clamped down to the table with a piece of scrap wood underneath to protect the table. Clamps in this careful operation should always be as close to the drilling as possible.

3. Attaching Inner Frame and Clips

After the holes are drilled and filed, set a rivet through the top hole of the back copper piece, with the rivet head on the etched side; place the top hole of the clip strip over the same rivet; then add one of the 19-inch strips. (See Fig. 300.) We are now ready to set our first rivet. Place your rivet set in your vise with the hollow for the rivet head just above the jaws of the vise. It is important to tighten the vise securely. At this point an extra pair of hands will make your task easier. Place your copper right side down so that the head of the rivet fits into the hollow of the rivet set. Have your strips in the position they will take when fastened. (See Fig. 301.) Proceed as on page 118 but do not tighten to the point of immobility. Repeat the same procedure at the bottom, adding the other 19-inch strip.

Now examine the folded clip strip. We shall need several more rivets to secure the clips properly against the back.

These rivets will be placed near the upper and lower sides of both sets of clips, but none will be necessary against the single fold at the bottom. (See Fig. 302.) The round heads of the rivets will appear on the right side along the middle scribed line. Follow the measurements given below for the placement of these rivets.

On the outside line, measure from the top edge; 1¼ inch, 2⅜ inches, 3⅝ inches, 4¾ inches. (See Fig. 303.) You will be using these same measurements exactly when you attach the side clips later. With your work set on a firm surface, just as before, center-punch these *four* marks exactly, and drill. (See Fig. 296.) Note in this case you are drilling through two pieces of copper, which assures accuracy of placement. File off burrs and set all rivets.

We are now ready to prepare our side clip strips. Scribe a line ¼ inch from, and parallel to, the hinges on each end of the back sheet. (See Fig. 304.) Measure down ¼ inch from the top edge, and ¼ inch up from the bottom on this line.

Mark these points accurately and repeat for the other two corners of your sheet. Clamp your 19-inch strip even with the top edge and drill your hole through the two thicknesses of copper. (See Fig. 305.) Clamp and drill the other three corners. At the right hand end of this same sheet, place your clip strip in its proper position, which is exactly that of the center strip already riveted. (See Fig. 306.) Center the strip on the drilled holes as you did before and clamp. Drill through the holes. With the clamps still in place, measure down from the top along the scribed lines near the hinges, the same measurements as those for the center back (1¼ inch, 2⅜ inches, 3⅝ inches, 4¾ inches). (See Fig. 303.) Center-punch and drill through both copper thicknesses. Now rivet the *four* middle rivets but *not* the top and bottom. (See Fig. 307.) There is still another step for the top and bottom holes before they are secured. Repeat all these steps in attaching the left hand clip.

You have now attached the clips which will hold the shelves in your cabinet. We must now re-attach our front sheet to the back with a temporary wire in the hinges.

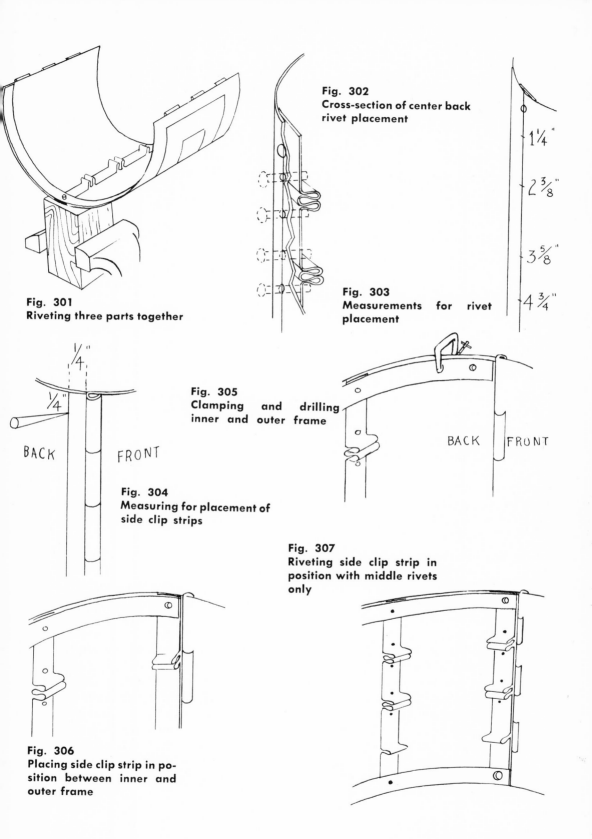

Fig. 301
Riveting three parts together

Fig. 302
Cross-section of center back
rivet placement

Fig. 303
Measurements for rivet
placement

1¼"

2⅜"

3⅝"

4¾"

¼"

¼"

BACK

FRONT

Fig. 304
Measuring for placement of
side clip strips

Fig. 305
Clamping and drilling
inner and outer frame

BACK   FRONT

Fig. 307
Riveting side clip strip in
position with middle rivets
only

Fig. 306
Placing side clip strip in position between inner and
outer frame

4. Attaching the Front Inner Frame

Take the 23-inch strip. Place it against the top edge of your front so that it overlaps the back about 2 inches on either side. (See Fig. 308.) Slide the ends of this strip behind the back 19-inch strip and the side clips, so that it is against the back sheet. (See Fig. 308.) Now clamp 1 inch from each end of the 23-inch strip to the back and to the 19-inch strips. Before going further, make sure that the 23-inch strip is flush against the front panel at all points. If necessary, loosen your clamps and readjust. Check also to be sure that the strip is flush with the top of the back sheet. You have already drilled holes through the top corners of your back sheet. Using this hole as a guide, drill through the 23-inch strip clamped to it. Repeat at opposite end of the back sheet. File burrs and secure rivets through all thicknesses (back sheet, 23-inch strip, clip strip, and 19-inch strip). Move clamps to the very end of the 23-inch strips, measure 1 inch from the hinge and ¼ inch from top of back sheet, make a mark. Center-punch and drill through back sheet, the 19-inch strip, and the 23-inch strip. (See Fig. 309.) Rivet and repeat at opposite ends of the 23-inch strip. Remove clamp. *Do not repeat* this whole operation yet, with your other 23-inch strip.

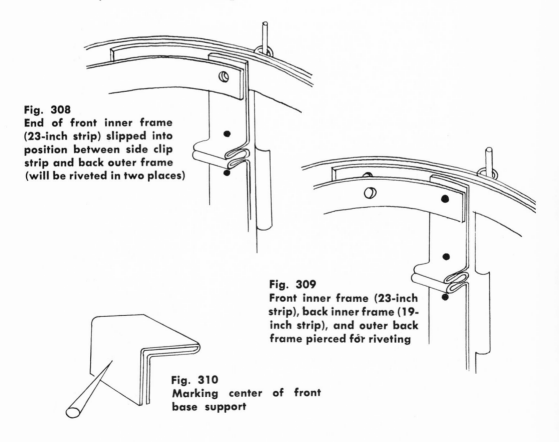

Fig. 308
End of front inner frame (23-inch strip) slipped into position between side clip strip and back outer frame (will be riveted in two places)

Fig. 309
Front inner frame (23-inch strip), back inner frame (19-inch strip), and outer back frame pierced for riveting

Fig. 310
Marking center of front base support

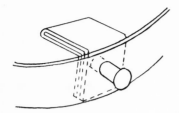

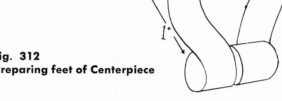

Fig. 311
Riveting front base support
to lower inner frame

Fig. 312
Preparing feet of Centerpiece

5. Riveting the Front Support

Now we must rivet in place the 2⅛-inch strip folded earlier. Measure up ¼ inch from the cut end and from each side of this strip. (See Fig. 310.) Make a mark, center-punch, and drill. Find the exact center from the ends of your lower, still unattached, 23-inch strip. One-fourth inch from the lower edge, mark, center-punch, and drill. Place the rivet through the hole in your 23-inch strip and then through the hole in the folded strip with the ledge facing away from the strip and the cut edge down. (See Fig. 311.) Rivet and set tight. Set aside for a moment the centerpiece and the strip just riveted.

6. Preparing the Feet

Take your piece of ½-inch dowel and your four 6⅛-inch (in length) strips. These feet are made exactly like the handles for the 13-inch plate, but with one coil less. They need not be in pairs; all roll in the same direction, but there will be a space from the end of the copper to the beginning of the coil of approximately 1 inch. (See Fig. 312.)

Take one of the legs and slip it under the center of the back sheet so that the two ends are inserted between the outer sheet and the 19-inch strip. (See Fig. 313.) Clamp them in place with your C clamps so that the top of the coil is ¼ inch below the lower rim of the centerpiece. (See Fig. 313.) You will find that the "up" ends protrude a bit above the 19-inch strip; with your scriber, mark on the protrusion a line even with the top of the 19-inch strip. Remove the foot, cut off the excess metal, and bevel that edge.

On the bottom edge of the back sheet of copper, measure ½ inch on each side of the center scribed line, and ¼ inch from the bottom edge. Mark these two points. Check to see whether the two ends of the leg strip are centered in relation to these two scribed points. If not even, stretch or compress the space between them until they fit. With your clamps firmly in place to the right and left of the leg (see Fig. 314), center-punch and drill and rivet through all three thicknesses of copper.

Take your 23-inch piece, upon which we riveted the one small ledge. Follow the same procedure as in the upper 23-inch strip for setting this in place along the lower edge. With one exception: put in only *one* rivet—the one which goes through the clip strip. (See Fig. 315.) The other rivet will be put in later with the foot. Do this at the opposite end as well.

Separate your hinges by withdrawing the temporary wire, and remove the front sheet.

The next foot to be attached is just below the hinge. The rivet which attaches the back part of the foot to the back sheet, and which is 1 inch back from the hinge and ¼ inch above the bottom edge, must also go through the 19-inch strip and the 23-inch strip as well as the back sheet. Slide this end of the foot between the 23-inch strip and the 19-inch strip; mark (see Fig. 315) on your back sheet 1 inch from the hinge and ¼ inch from the bottom edge. See that the end of the strip from the foot is centered upon that mark and that the top of the coil is ¼ inch from the bottom rim of the centerpiece as in the previously riveted foot. (See Fig. 315.)

At this point, compare the two feet. Place C clamps on both sides of the place to be drilled and riveted. Before center-punching, check all measurements again. Then center-punch, drill, mark off any protrusion, cut to fit, and file, before riveting securely. Follow the same steps for the foot at the opposite side, behind the other hinge.

With the front sheet off, the unriveted ends of both feet just attached must be placed on the inside of the 23-inch strip. (See Fig. 315.) Measuring on the 23-inch strip, a mark should be made ¼ inch from the lower edge of the strip and ½ inch from the closest rivet. Clamp the loose end of the foot in place so that it is centered on that mark and so that the top of the coil is ¼ inch from and parallel to the bottom edge of the centerpiece. (See Fig. 316.) Mark, center-punch, drill, file, and rivet. Do the same for the loose end of the opposite foot.

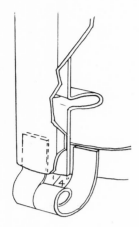

Fig. 313
Setting center back foot in place between lower inner frame and outer frame

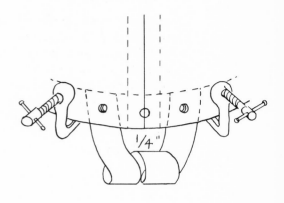

Fig. 314
Riveting back foot in place

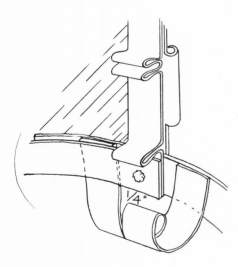

Fig. 315
Setting side foot in place

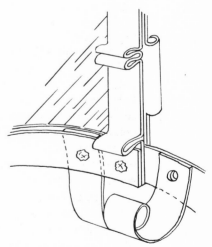

Fig. 316
Riveting one end of side foot to back section (second end of foot will be riveted when front outer frame is removed)

7. Attaching the Fourth Foot

At the center front of the 23-inch strip, measure ½ inch to either side of the rivet, ¼ inch from the bottom edge of this strip; make a mark crossing the ½-inch marks just scribed. Where these two marks cross, center-punch, drill, and file, as shown in Fig. 317. Place the two ends of the remaining foot behind the 23-inch strip (see Fig. 317) and with the same measurements used in placing the other three feet, hold carefully and with the scriber, mark a circle through the holes already drilled. Center-punch, drill, file, and check for protrusion of foot ends above the 23-inch strip. Cut and bevel smooth before riveting the foot securely in place.

8. Preparing Inside Base

Prepare your 12-inch disk by beveling the edge. Turn your centerpiece frame upside down. There are four ledges facing into the center. On each of these, measure from the folded edge and from both sides ¼ inch in to get your center. Center-punch and drill through both thicknesses of metal on each of your ledges, as seen in Fig. 318. File. With your centerpiece still inverted, press your 12-inch disk under the *four* drilled ledges, so that when the whole piece is set upright this disk will be resting on them. (See Fig. 318.)

Your first step in attaching the disk to these ledges will be riveting only ledges A and B indicated in Fig. 318. On your disk, mark the position of the holes on A and B by scribing through them onto the disk. Remove the disk, center-punch the two holes, and drill. File and rivet securely in place. The head of the rivet should be *under* the disk so that it will be on top when the piece is rightside up. The disk should just touch on the outside surface of the lower 23-inch strip. You will need help in marking the second pair of holes in your 12-inch disk. You will find a gap at the hinged sides of your centerpiece. The gap between the 12-inch disk and the hinges must be closed by hand pressure while you insert the drill in the holes through the two ledges and drill through the disk. (See Fig. 319.) File and rivet.

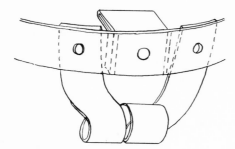

Fig. 317
Front foot and inner frame
pierced for riveting

Fig. 318
Placing base _under_ sup-
ports in overturned Centerpiece

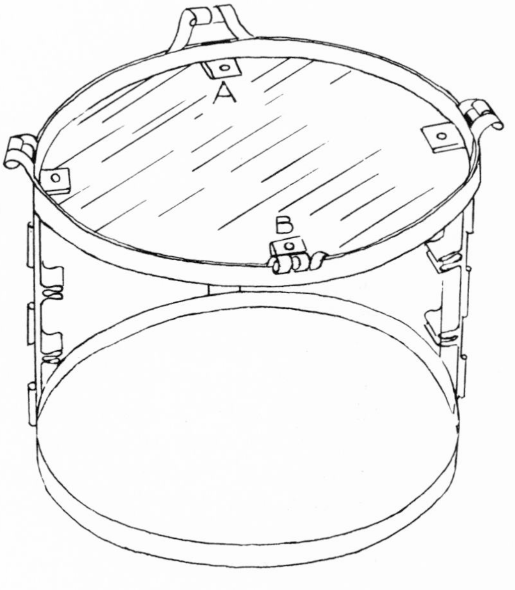

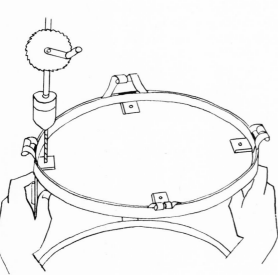

Fig. 319
Pressing hinged sides in,
for piercing of base and
supports

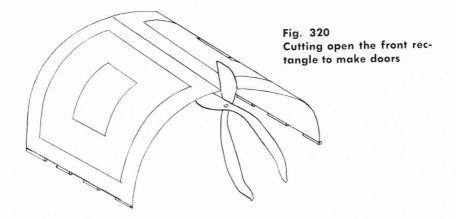

Fig. 320
Cutting open the front rectangle to make doors

9. Cutting the Front Doors

Now take your front sheet and cut very carefully along the scribed line in the center with either the jeweler's saw or the tinsnips. Use the tool with which you are most accurate. (See Fig. 320.) This is the front of your doors. Bevel the edges you have just cut, removing as little material as possible. You are now ready to use a fresh piece of wire 12 inches long and assemble your hinge. Allow your wire to go through your hinge, beginning at the top and extending out the bottom, for 1 inch. Do this on both hinges. Bend the top of your hinge wires over the top edge of your piece. Fold the wire down flat over and against the 23-inch strip and against the end of the 19-inch strip. Tap down with the buckskin mallet against the frame. (See Fig. 321.) Do the same with the lower ends of the wire. If ends protrude when the door is open, file them off and smooth with steel wool.

Fig. 321
Ends of permanent hinge wire fold down against inner frame

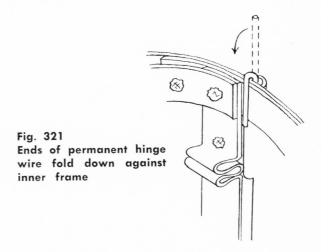

Fig. 322
Hasp—exact size

10. The Hasp

To fasten the front doors, you'll need a small hasp. On this page is a diagram which is drawn to exact size. (Fig. 322.) Copy this on tracing paper. Cut a strip of copper ⅜ inch x 1¼ inches. Measure in from the left edge ⅛ inch and down from the top ³⁄₁₆ inch. Mark, center-punch, and drill this hole. (See Fig. 323.) Do the same at the other end of the strip. Now cement the pattern to your piece of copper with rubber cement and cut it out with a jeweler's saw. You will find that you cut into the hole on the right end, which is correct. File and smooth all edges.

11. Attaching the Hasp

Now measure in from the side on each door ⅜ inch and 4 inches from the bottom. Where these marks cross, center-punch, drill, and file. Now insert the rivets loosely enough to allow the hasp to swing and catch on the opposite

Fig. 323
Marking and drilling a hole
at each end

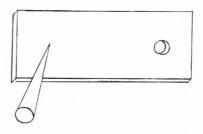

side. Achieve this by doing the following: Place a rivet through the hole in the left-hand side of the hasp. (See Fig. 324.) Cut a couple of inches off your test wire. With your round-nose pliers, make an open loop large enough to fit over your rivet with a tight fit. (See Fig. 325.) Put your rivet with the hasp and wire through the hole in the left-hand door. (See Fig. 326.) Turn your door so the rivet head fits in the hollow of your rivet stake, and rivet as usual—being careful to see that the wire stays in position while riveting. Remove your wire. The rivet should be anchored, but loose. (See Fig. 327.) Wrap two turns of wire around the stem of another rivet (see Fig. 328) and push it through the hole in the right-hand door. Rivet as usual, and unwrap the wire. This rivet is anchored, but is also loose.

Clean your serving centerpiece, oxidize it, and clean it again, highlighting the smooth surfaces and leaving enough oxidizing in the design for character.

If you wish, when you are sure you like the polish and the oxidizing of your piece, spray the centerpiece with lacquer.

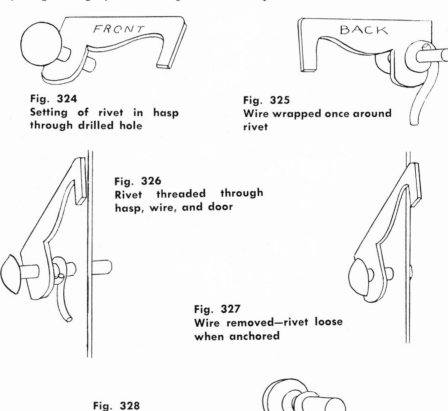

Fig. 324
Setting of rivet in hasp through drilled hole

Fig. 325
Wire wrapped once around rivet

Fig. 326
Rivet threaded through hasp, wire, and door

Fig. 327
Wire removed—rivet loose when anchored

Fig. 328
Two turns of wire around rivet on right hand door, to leave rivet loose when anchored

Chapter 14

CONCLUSION

In presenting these projects, emphasis throughout has been on releasing the spirit through creative activity.

It is important to know that you are capable of making beautiful things —that methods are just roads to take you anywhere you choose.

As craftsmen, we have taken the middle road in design, and we hope we have left you free. With these techniques at your command, design for you can take on the sleek lines of the modern, or the more intricate traditional. With the skills you have acquired and the valuable basic collection of tools you have accumulated, you are well set.

As a craftsman, you may now follow your own bent. Have the courage to try things out and give form to your own individual expression.

Some Sources of Supply

American Handicrafts Company—Tandy Leather ⸻⸻ Cut copper and
705 Throckmorton St., Fort Worth, Texas 76102   other materials

and these branches (list not complete, check your local directory):

Alabama, Birmingham
1020 S. 20th St. 35210

New York, New York
384 Fifth Ave. 10017

California, San Francisco
1310 Mission St. 94103

New York, New York
115 W. 45th St. 10036

Illinois, Chicago
5945 47th St. W. 60638

New York, New York
20 W. 14th St. 10011

Iowa, Davenport
3628 Bridge Ave. 52807

Oklahoma, Tulsa
5010 S. Sheridan Rd. 74145

Minnesota, Minneapolis
1105 Nicollet Ave. S. 55403

Pennsylvania, Philadelphia
124 S. 13th St. 19107

Missouri, St. Louis
135 Concord Plaza Shopping Center 63128

Utah, Salt Lake City
164 E. 2nd St. 84111

New York, Albany
85 Central Ave. 12206

Washington, Seattle
2026 Third Ave. 98121

T. E. Conklin Brass and Copper Co. ⸻⸻ Sheet copper
324 W. 23rd St., New York, N. Y. 10011

William Dixon Inc. ⸻⸻ Tools, mordants
750 Washington Ave., Carlstadt, N. J. 07072

Charles Dorsch & Son ⸻⸻ Molds
4462 28th St., Detroit, Mich. 48210

Handy and Harman ⸻⸻ Silver
Office: 850 Third Ave., New York, N. Y. 10022
Store: 7 E. 47th St., New York, N. Y. 10017

A CATALOGUE OF SELECTED DOVER BOOKS
IN ALL FIELDS OF INTEREST

A CATALOGUE OF SELECTED DOVER BOOKS
IN ALL FIELDS OF INTEREST

AMERICA'S OLD MASTERS, James T. Flexner. Four men emerged unexpectedly from provincial 18th century America to leadership in European art: Benjamin West, J. S. Copley, C. R. Peale, Gilbert Stuart. Brilliant coverage of lives and contributions. Revised, 1967 edition. 69 plates. 365pp. of text.

21806-6 Paperbound $3.00

FIRST FLOWERS OF OUR WILDERNESS: AMERICAN PAINTING, THE COLONIAL PERIOD, James T. Flexner. Painters, and regional painting traditions from earliest Colonial times up to the emergence of Copley, West and Peale Sr., Foster, Gustavus Hesselius, Feke, John Smibert and many anonymous painters in the primitive manner. Engaging presentation, with 162 illustrations. xxii + 368pp.

22180-6 Paperbound $3.50

THE LIGHT OF DISTANT SKIES: AMERICAN PAINTING, 1760-1835, James T. Flexner. The great generation of early American painters goes to Europe to learn and to teach: West, Copley, Gilbert Stuart and others. Allston, Trumbull, Morse; also contemporary American painters—primitives, derivatives, academics—who remained in America. 102 illustrations. xiii + 306pp.   22179-2 Paperbound $3.00

A HISTORY OF THE RISE AND PROGRESS OF THE ARTS OF DESIGN IN THE UNITED STATES, William Dunlap. Much the richest mine of information on early American painters, sculptors, architects, engravers, miniaturists, etc. The only source of information for scores of artists, the major primary source for many others. Unabridged reprint of rare original 1834 edition, with new introduction by James T. Flexner, and 394 new illustrations. Edited by Rita Weiss. 6⅝ x 9⅝.

21695-0, 21696-9, 21697-7 Three volumes, Paperbound $13.50

EPOCHS OF CHINESE AND JAPANESE ART, Ernest F. Fenollosa. From primitive Chinese art to the 20th century, thorough history, explanation of every important art period and form, including Japanese woodcuts; main stress on China and Japan, but Tibet, Korea also included. Still unexcelled for its detailed, rich coverage of cultural background, aesthetic elements, diffusion studies, particularly of the historical period. 2nd, 1913 edition. 242 illustrations. lii + 439pp. of text.

20364-6, 20365-4 Two volumes, Paperbound $6.00

THE GENTLE ART OF MAKING ENEMIES, James A. M. Whistler. Greatest wit of his day deflates Oscar Wilde, Ruskin, Swinburne; strikes back at inane critics, exhibitions, art journalism; aesthetics of impressionist revolution in most striking form. Highly readable classic by great painter. Reproduction of edition designed by Whistler. Introduction by Alfred Werner. xxxvi + 334pp.

21875-9 Paperbound $2.50

VISUAL ILLUSIONS: THEIR CAUSES, CHARACTERISTICS, AND APPLICATIONS, Matthew Luckiesh. Thorough description and discussion of optical illusion, geometric and perspective, particularly; size and shape distortions, illusions of color, of motion; natural illusions; use of illusion in art and magic, industry, etc. Most useful today with op art, also for classical art. Scores of effects illustrated. Introduction by William H. Ittleson. 100 illustrations. xxi + 252pp.

21530-X Paperbound $2.00

A HANDBOOK OF ANATOMY FOR ART STUDENTS, Arthur Thomson. Thorough, virtually exhaustive coverage of skeletal structure, musculature, etc. Full text, supplemented by anatomical diagrams and drawings and by photographs of undraped figures. Unique in its comparison of male and female forms, pointing out differences of contour, texture, form. 211 figures, 40 drawings, 86 photographs. xx + 459pp. 5⅜ x 8⅜. 21163-0 Paperbound $3.50

150 MASTERPIECES OF DRAWING, Selected by Anthony Toney. Full page reproductions of drawings from the early 16th to the end of the 18th century, all beautifully reproduced: Rembrandt, Michelangelo, Dürer, Fragonard, Urs, Graf, Wouwerman, many others. First-rate browsing book, model book for artists. xviii + 150pp. 8⅜ x 11¼. 21032-4 Paperbound $2.50

THE LATER WORK OF AUBREY BEARDSLEY, Aubrey Beardsley. Exotic, erotic, ironic masterpieces in full maturity: Comedy Ballet, Venus and Tannhauser, Pierrot, Lysistrata, Rape of the Lock, Savoy material, Ali Baba, Volpone, etc. This material revolutionized the art world, and is still powerful, fresh, brilliant. With *The Early Work,* all Beardsley's finest work. 174 plates, 2 in color. xiv + 176pp. 8⅛ x 11. 21817-1 Paperbound $3.00

DRAWINGS OF REMBRANDT, Rembrandt van Rijn. Complete reproduction of fabulously rare edition by Lippmann and Hofstede de Groot, completely reedited, updated, improved by Prof. Seymour Slive, Fogg Museum. Portraits, Biblical sketches, landscapes, Oriental types, nudes, episodes from classical mythology—All Rembrandt's fertile genius. Also selection of drawings by his pupils and followers. "Stunning volumes," *Saturday Review.* 550 illustrations. lxxviii + 552pp. 9⅛ x 12¼. 21485-0, 21486-9 Two volumes, Paperbound $7.00

THE DISASTERS OF WAR, Francisco Goya. One of the masterpieces of Western civilization—83 etchings that record Goya's shattering, bitter reaction to the Napoleonic war that swept through Spain after the insurrection of 1808 and to war in general. Reprint of the first edition, with three additional plates from Boston's Museum of Fine Arts. All plates facsimile size. Introduction by Philip Hofer, Fogg Museum. v + 97pp. 9⅜ x 8¼. 21872-4 Paperbound $2.00

GRAPHIC WORKS OF ODILON REDON. Largest collection of Redon's graphic works ever assembled: 172 lithographs, 28 etchings and engravings, 9 drawings. These include some of his most famous works. All the plates from *Odilon Redon: oeuvre graphique complet,* plus additional plates. New introduction and caption translations by Alfred Werner. 209 illustrations. xxvii + 209pp. 9⅛ x 12¼. 21966-8 Paperbound $4.00

DESIGN BY ACCIDENT; A BOOK OF "ACCIDENTAL EFFECTS" FOR ARTISTS AND DESIGNERS, James F. O'Brien. Create your own unique, striking, imaginative effects by "controlled accident" interaction of materials: paints and lacquers, oil and water based paints, splatter, crackling materials, shatter, similar items. Everything you do will be different; first book on this limitless art, so useful to both fine artist and commercial artist. Full instructions. 192 plates showing "accidents," 8 in color. viii + 215pp. 8⅜ x 11¼.   21942-9 Paperbound $3.50

THE BOOK OF SIGNS, Rudolf Koch. Famed German type designer draws 493 beautiful symbols: religious, mystical, alchemical, imperial, property marks, runes, etc. Remarkable fusion of traditional and modern. Good for suggestions of timelessness, smartness, modernity. Text. vi + 104pp. 6⅛ x 9¼.
                                            20162-7 Paperbound $1.25

HISTORY OF INDIAN AND INDONESIAN ART, Ananda K. Coomaraswamy. An unabridged republication of one of the finest books by a great scholar in Eastern art. Rich in descriptive material, history, social backgrounds; Sunga reliefs, Rajput paintings, Gupta temples, Burmese frescoes, textiles, jewelry, sculpture, etc. 400 photos. viii + 423pp. 6⅜ x 9¾.   21436-2 Paperbound $4.00

PRIMITIVE ART, Franz Boas. America's foremost anthropologist surveys textiles, ceramics, woodcarving, basketry, metalwork, etc.; patterns, technology, creation of symbols, style origins. All areas of world, but very full on Northwest Coast Indians. More than 350 illustrations of baskets, boxes, totem poles, weapons, etc. 378 pp.
                                            20025-6 Paperbound $3.00

THE GENTLEMAN AND CABINET MAKER'S DIRECTOR, Thomas Chippendale. Full reprint (third edition, 1762) of most influential furniture book of all time, by master cabinetmaker. 200 plates, illustrating chairs, sofas, mirrors, tables, cabinets, plus 24 photographs of surviving pieces. Biographical introduction by N. Bienenstock. vi + 249pp. 9⅞ x 12¾.   21601-2 Paperbound $4.00

AMERICAN ANTIQUE FURNITURE, Edgar G. Miller, Jr. The basic coverage of all American furniture before 1840. Individual chapters cover type of furniture— clocks, tables, sideboards, etc.—chronologically, with inexhaustible wealth of data. More than 2100 photographs, all identified, commented on. Essential to all early American collectors. Introduction by H. E. Keyes. vi + 1106pp. 7⅞ x 10¾.
               21599-7, 21600-4 Two volumes, Paperbound $11.00

PENNSYLVANIA DUTCH AMERICAN FOLK ART, Henry J. Kauffman. 279 photos, 28 drawings of tulipware, Fraktur script, painted tinware, toys, flowered furniture, quilts, samplers, hex signs, house interiors, etc. Full descriptive text. Excellent for tourist, rewarding for designer, collector. Map. 146pp. 7⅞ x 10¾.
                                            21205-X Paperbound $2.50

EARLY NEW ENGLAND GRAVESTONE RUBBINGS, Edmund V. Gillon, Jr. 43 photographs, 226 carefully reproduced rubbings show heavily symbolic, sometimes macabre early gravestones, up to early 19th century. Remarkable early American primitive art, occasionally strikingly beautiful; always powerful. Text. xxvi + 207pp. 8⅜ x 11¼.   21380-3 Paperbound $3.50

ALPHABETS AND ORNAMENTS, Ernst Lehner. Well-known pictorial source for decorative alphabets, script examples, cartouches, frames, decorative title pages, calligraphic initials, borders, similar material. 14th to 19th century, mostly European. Useful in almost any graphic arts designing, varied styles. 750 illustrations. 256pp. 7 x 10.   21905-4 Paperbound $4.00

PAINTING: A CREATIVE APPROACH, Norman Colquhoun. For the beginner simple guide provides an instructive approach to painting: major stumbling blocks for beginner; overcoming them, technical points; paints and pigments; oil painting; watercolor and other media and color. New section on "plastic" paints. Glossary. Formerly *Paint Your Own Pictures*. 221pp.   22000-1 Paperbound $1.75

THE ENJOYMENT AND USE OF COLOR, Walter Sargent. Explanation of the relations between colors themselves and between colors in nature and art, including hundreds of little-known facts about color values, intensities, effects of high and low illumination, complementary colors. Many practical hints for painters, references to great masters. 7 color plates, 29 illustrations. x + 274pp.
20944-X Paperbound $2.50

THE NOTEBOOKS OF LEONARDO DA VINCI, compiled and edited by Jean Paul Richter. 1566 extracts from original manuscripts reveal the full range of Leonardo's versatile genius: all his writings on painting, sculpture, architecture, anatomy, astronomy, geography, topography, physiology, mining, music, etc., in both Italian and English, with 186 plates of manuscript pages and more than 500 additional drawings. Includes studies for the Last Supper, the lost Sforza monument, and other works. Total of xlvii + 866pp. 7⅞ x 10¾.
22572-0, 22573-9 Two volumes, Paperbound $10.00

MONTGOMERY WARD CATALOGUE OF 1895. Tea gowns, yards of flannel and pillow-case lace, stereoscopes, books of gospel hymns, the New Improved Singer Sewing Machine, side saddles, milk skimmers, straight-edged razors, high-button shoes, spittoons, and on and on . . . listing some 25,000 items, practically all illustrated. Essential to the shoppers of the 1890's, it is our truest record of the spirit of the period. Unaltered reprint of Issue No. 57, Spring and Summer 1895. Introduction by Boris Emmet. Innumerable illustrations. xiii + 624pp. 8½ x 11⅝.
22377-9 Paperbound $6.95

THE CRYSTAL PALACE EXHIBITION ILLUSTRATED CATALOGUE (LONDON, 1851). One of the wonders of the modern world—the Crystal Palace Exhibition in which all the nations of the civilized world exhibited their achievements in the arts and sciences—presented in an equally important illustrated catalogue. More than 1700 items pictured with accompanying text—ceramics, textiles, cast-iron work, carpets, pianos, sleds, razors, wall-papers, billiard tables, beehives, silverware and hundreds of other artifacts—represent the focal point of Victorian culture in the Western World. Probably the largest collection of Victorian decorative art ever assembled— indispensable for antiquarians and designers. Unabridged republication of the Art-Journal Catalogue of the Great Exhibition of 1851, with all terminal essays. New introduction by John Gloag, F.S.A. xxxiv + 426pp. 9 x 12.
22503-8 Paperbound $4.50

A HISTORY OF COSTUME, Carl Köhler. Definitive history, based on surviving pieces of clothing primarily, and paintings, statues, etc. secondarily. Highly readable text, supplemented by 594 illustrations of costumes of the ancient Mediterranean peoples, Greece and Rome, the Teutonic prehistoric period; costumes of the Middle Ages, Renaissance, Baroque, 18th and 19th centuries. Clear, measured patterns are provided for many clothing articles. Approach is practical throughout. Enlarged by Emma von Sichart. 464pp.   21030-8 Paperbound $3.50

ORIENTAL RUGS, ANTIQUE AND MODERN, Walter A. Hawley. A complete and authoritative treatise on the Oriental rug—where they are made, by whom and how, designs and symbols, characteristics in detail of the six major groups, how to distinguish them and how to buy them. Detailed technical data is provided on periods, weaves, warps, wefts, textures, sides, ends and knots, although no technical background is required for an understanding. 11 color plates, 80 halftones, 4 maps. vi + 320pp. 6⅛ x 9⅛.   22366-3 Paperbound $5.00

TEN BOOKS ON ARCHITECTURE, Vitruvius. By any standards the most important book on architecture ever written. Early Roman discussion of aesthetics of building, construction methods, orders, sites, and every other aspect of architecture has inspired, instructed architecture for about 2,000 years. Stands behind Palladio, Michelangelo, Bramante, Wren, countless others. Definitive Morris H. Morgan translation. 68 illustrations. xii + 331pp.   20645-9 Paperbound $2.50

THE FOUR BOOKS OF ARCHITECTURE, Andrea Palladio. Translated into every major Western European language in the two centuries following its publication in 1570, this has been one of the most influential books in the history of architecture. Complete reprint of the 1738 Isaac Ware edition. New introduction by Adolf Placzek, Columbia Univ. 216 plates. xxii + 110pp. of text. 9½ x 12¾.
                            21308-0 Clothbound $10.00

STICKS AND STONES: A STUDY OF AMERICAN ARCHITECTURE AND CIVILIZATION, Lewis Mumford.One of the great classics of American cultural history. American architecture from the medieval-inspired earliest forms to the early 20th century; evolution of structure and style, and reciprocal influences on environment. 21 photographic illustrations. 238pp.   20202-X Paperbound $2.00

THE AMERICAN BUILDER'S COMPANION, Asher Benjamin. The most widely used early 19th century architectural style and source book, for colonial up into Greek Revival periods. Extensive development of geometry of carpentering, construction of sashes, frames, doors, stairs; plans and elevations of domestic and other buildings. Hundreds of thousands of houses were built according to this book, now invaluable to historians, architects, restorers, etc. 1827 edition. 59 plates. 114pp. 7⅞ x 10¾.
                            22236-5 Paperbound $3.00

DUTCH HOUSES IN THE HUDSON VALLEY BEFORE 1776, Helen Wilkinson Reynolds. The standard survey of the Dutch colonial house and outbuildings, with constructional features, decoration, and local history associated with individual homesteads. Introduction by Franklin D. Roosevelt. Map. 150 illustrations. 469pp. 6⅝ x 9¼.   21469-9 Paperbound $4.00

JOHANN SEBASTIAN BACH, Philipp Spitta. One of the great classics of musicology, this definitive analysis of Bach's music (and life) has never been surpassed. Lucid, nontechnical analyses of hundreds of pieces (30 pages devoted to St. Matthew Passion, 26 to B Minor Mass). Also includes major analysis of 18th-century music. 450 musical examples. 40-page musical supplement. Total of xx + 1799pp.
(EUK) 22278-0, 22279-9 Two volumes, Clothbound $15.00

MOZART AND HIS PIANO CONCERTOS, Cuthbert Girdlestone. The only full-length study of an important area of Mozart's creativity. Provides detailed analyses of all 23 concertos, traces inspirational sources. 417 musical examples. Second edition. 509pp.
(USO) 21271-8 Paperbound $3.50

THE PERFECT WAGNERITE: A COMMENTARY ON THE NIBLUNG'S RING, George Bernard Shaw. Brilliant and still relevant criticism in remarkable essays on Wagner's Ring cycle, Shaw's ideas on political and social ideology behind the plots, role of Leitmotifs, vocal requisites, etc. Prefaces. xxi + 136pp.
21707-8 Paperbound $1.50

DON GIOVANNI, W. A. Mozart. Complete libretto, modern English translation; biographies of composer and librettist; accounts of early performances and critical reaction. Lavishly illustrated. All the material you need to understand and appreciate this great work. Dover Opera Guide and Libretto Series; translated and introduced by Ellen Bleiler. 92 illustrations. 209pp.
21134-7 Paperbound $1.50

HIGH FIDELITY SYSTEMS: A LAYMAN'S GUIDE, Roy F. Allison. All the basic information you need for setting up your own audio system: high fidelity and stereo record players, tape records, F.M. Connections, adjusting tone arm, cartridge, checking needle alignment, positioning speakers, phasing speakers, adjusting hums, trouble-shooting, maintenance, and similar topics. Enlarged 1965 edition. More than 50 charts, diagrams, photos. iv + 91pp.   21514-8 Paperbound $1.25

REPRODUCTION OF SOUND, Edgar Villchur. Thorough coverage for laymen of high fidelity systems, reproducing systems in general, needles, amplifiers, preamps, loudspeakers, feedback, explaining physical background. "A rare talent for making technicalities vividly comprehensible," R. Darrell, *High Fidelity*. 69 figures. iv + 92pp.   21515-6 Paperbound $1.00

HEAR ME TALKIN' TO YA: THE STORY OF JAZZ AS TOLD BY THE MEN WHO MADE IT, Nat Shapiro and Nat Hentoff. Louis Armstrong, Fats Waller, Jo Jones, Clarence Williams, Billy Holiday, Duke Ellington, Jelly Roll Morton and dozens of other jazz greats tell how it was in Chicago's South Side, New Orleans, depression Harlem and the modern West Coast as jazz was born and grew. xvi + 429pp.
21726-4 Paperbound $2.50

FABLES OF AESOP, translated by Sir Roger L'Estrange. A reproduction of the very rare 1931 Paris edition; a selection of the most interesting fables, together with 50 imaginative drawings by Alexander Calder. v + 128pp. 6½x9¼.
21780-9 Paperbound $1.25

POEMS OF ANNE BRADSTREET, edited with an introduction by Robert Hutchinson. A new selection of poems by America's first poet and perhaps the first significant woman poet in the English language. 48 poems display her development in works of considerable variety—love poems, domestic poems, religious meditations, formal elegies, "quaternions," etc. Notes, bibliography. viii + 222pp.
22160-1 Paperbound $2.00

THREE GOTHIC NOVELS: THE CASTLE OF OTRANTO BY HORACE WALPOLE; VATHEK BY WILLIAM BECKFORD; THE VAMPYRE BY JOHN POLIDORI, WITH FRAGMENT OF A NOVEL BY LORD BYRON, edited by E. F. Bleiler. The first Gothic novel, by Walpole; the finest Oriental tale in English, by Beckford; powerful Romantic supernatural story in versions by Polidori and Byron. All extremely important in history of literature; all still exciting, packed with supernatural thrills, ghosts, haunted castles, magic, etc. xl + 291pp.
21232-7 Paperbound $2.00

THE BEST TALES OF HOFFMANN, E. T. A. Hoffmann. 10 of Hoffmann's most important stories, in modern re-editings of standard translations: Nutcracker and the King of Mice, Signor Formica, Automata, The Sandman, Rath Krespel, The Golden Flowerpot, Master Martin the Cooper, The Mines of Falun, The King's Betrothed, A New Year's Eve Adventure. 7 illustrations by Hoffmann. Edited by E. F. Bleiler. xxxix + 419pp.
21793-0 Paperbound $2.50

GHOST AND HORROR STORIES OF AMBROSE BIERCE, Ambrose Bierce. 23 strikingly modern stories of the horrors latent in the human mind: The Eyes of the Panther, The Damned Thing, An Occurrence at Owl Creek Bridge, An Inhabitant of Carcosa, etc., plus the dream-essay, Visions of the Night. Edited by E. F. Bleiler. xxii + 199pp.
20767-6 Paperbound $1.50

BEST GHOST STORIES OF J. S. LeFANU, J. Sheridan LeFanu. Finest stories by Victorian master often considered greatest supernatural writer of all. Carmilla, Green Tea, The Haunted Baronet, The Familiar, and 12 others. Most never before available in the U. S. A. Edited by E. F. Bleiler. 8 illustrations from Victorian publications. xvii + 467pp.
20415-4 Paperbound $2.50

THE TIME STREAM, THE GREATEST ADVENTURE, AND THE PURPLE SAPPHIRE— THREE SCIENCE FICTION NOVELS, John Taine (Eric Temple Bell). Great American mathematician was also foremost science fiction novelist of the 1920's. *The Time Stream,* one of all-time classics, uses concepts of circular time; *The Greatest Adventure,* incredibly ancient biological experiments from Antarctica threaten to escape; The *Purple Sapphire,* superscience, lost races in Central Tibet, survivors of the Great Race. 4 illustrations by Frank R. Paul. v + 532pp.
21180-0 Paperbound $3.00

SEVEN SCIENCE FICTION NOVELS, H. G. Wells. The standard collection of the great novels. Complete, unabridged. *First Men in the Moon, Island of Dr. Moreau, War of the Worlds, Food of the Gods, Invisible Man, Time Machine, In the Days of the Comet.* Not only science fiction fans, but every educated person owes it to himself to read these novels. 1015pp.
20264-X Clothbound $5.00

THE RED FAIRY BOOK, Andrew Lang. Lang's color fairy books have long been children's favorites. This volume includes Rapunzel, Jack and the Bean-stalk and 35 other stories, familiar and unfamiliar. 4 plates, 93 illustrations x + 367pp.
21673-X Paperbound $2.50

THE BLUE FAIRY BOOK, Andrew Lang. Lang's tales come from all countries and all times. Here are 37 tales from Grimm, the Arabian Nights, Greek Mythology, and other fascinating sources. 8 plates, 130 illustrations. xi + 390pp.
21437-0 Paperbound $2.50

HOUSEHOLD STORIES BY THE BROTHERS GRIMM. Classic English-language edition of the well-known tales — Rumpelstiltskin, Snow White, Hansel and Gretel, The Twelve Brothers, Faithful John, Rapunzel, Tom Thumb (52 stories in all). Translated into simple, straightforward English by Lucy Crane. Ornamented with headpieces, vignettes, elaborate decorative initials and a dozen full-page illustrations by Walter Crane. x + 269pp.
21080-4 Paperbound $2.50

THE MERRY ADVENTURES OF ROBIN HOOD, Howard Pyle. The finest modern versions of the traditional ballads and tales about the great English outlaw. Howard Pyle's complete prose version, with every word, every illustration of the first edition. Do not confuse this facsimile of the original (1883) with modern editions that change text or illustrations. 23 plates plus many page decorations. xxii + 296pp.
22043-5 Paperbound $2.50

THE STORY OF KING ARTHUR AND HIS KNIGHTS, Howard Pyle. The finest children's version of the life of King Arthur; brilliantly retold by Pyle, with 48 of his most imaginative illustrations. xviii + 313pp. 6⅛ x 9¼.
21445-1 Paperbound $2.50

THE WONDERFUL WIZARD OF OZ, L. Frank Baum. America's finest children's book in facsimile of first edition with all Denslow illustrations in full color. The edition a child should have. Introduction by Martin Gardner. 23 color plates, scores of drawings. iv + 267pp.
20691-2 Paperbound $2.25

THE MARVELOUS LAND OF OZ, L. Frank Baum. The second Oz book, every bit as imaginative as the Wizard. The hero is a boy named Tip, but the Scarecrow and the Tin Woodman are back, as is the Oz magic. 16 color plates, 120 drawings by John R. Neill. 287pp.
20692-0 Paperbound $2.50

THE MAGICAL MONARCH OF MO, L. Frank Baum. Remarkable adventures in a land even stranger than Oz. The best of Baum's books not in the Oz series. 15 color plates and dozens of drawings by Frank Verbeck. xviii + 237pp.
21892-9 Paperbound $2.00

THE BAD CHILD'S BOOK OF BEASTS, MORE BEASTS FOR WORSE CHILDREN, A MORAL ALPHABET, Hilaire Belloc. Three complete humor classics in one volume. Be kind to the frog, and do not call him names . . . and 28 other whimsical animals. Familiar favorites and some not so well known. Illustrated by Basil Blackwell. 156pp.
(USO) 20749-8 Paperbound $1.25

EAST O' THE SUN AND WEST O' THE MOON, George W. Dasent. Considered the best of all translations of these Norwegian folk tales, this collection has been enjoyed by generations of children (and folklorists too). Includes True and Untrue, Why the Sea is Salt, East O' the Sun and West O' the Moon, Why the Bear is Stumpy-Tailed, Boots and the Troll, The Cock and the Hen, Rich Peter the Pedlar, and 52 more. The only edition with all 59 tales. 77 illustrations by Erik Werenskiold and Theodor Kittelsen. xv + 418pp. 22521-6 Paperbound $3.00

GOOPS AND HOW TO BE THEM, Gelett Burgess. Classic of tongue-in-cheek humor, masquerading as etiquette book. 87 verses, twice as many cartoons, show mischievous Goops as they demonstrate to children virtues of table manners, neatness, courtesy, etc. Favorite for generations. viii + 88pp. 6½ x 9¼. 22233-0 Paperbound $1.25

ALICE'S ADVENTURES UNDER GROUND, Lewis Carroll. The first version, quite different from the final *Alice in Wonderland,* printed out by Carroll himself with his own illustrations. Complete facsimile of the "million dollar" manuscript Carroll gave to Alice Liddell in 1864. Introduction by Martin Gardner. viii + 96pp. Title and dedication pages in color. 21482-6 Paperbound $1.25

THE BROWNIES, THEIR BOOK, Palmer Cox. Small as mice, cunning as foxes, exuberant and full of mischief, the Brownies go to the zoo, toy shop, seashore, circus, etc., in 24 verse adventures and 266 illustrations. Long a favorite, since their first appearance in St. Nicholas Magazine. xi + 144pp. 6⅝ x 9¼. 21265-3 Paperbound $1.75

SONGS OF CHILDHOOD, Walter De La Mare. Published (under the pseudonym Walter Ramal) when De La Mare was only 29, this charming collection has long been a favorite children's book. A facsimile of the first edition in paper, the 47 poems capture the simplicity of the nursery rhyme and the ballad, including such lyrics as I Met Eve, Tartary, The Silver Penny. vii + 106pp. 21972-0 Paperbound $1.25

THE COMPLETE NONSENSE OF EDWARD LEAR, Edward Lear. The finest 19th-century humorist-cartoonist in full: all nonsense limericks, zany alphabets, Owl and Pussycat, songs, nonsense botany, and more than 500 illustrations by Lear himself. Edited by Holbrook Jackson. xxix + 287pp. (USO) 20167-8 Paperbound $2.00

BILLY WHISKERS: THE AUTOBIOGRAPHY OF A GOAT, Frances Trego Montgomery. A favorite of children since the early 20th century, here are the escapades of that rambunctious, irresistible and mischievous goat—Billy Whiskers. Much in the spirit of *Peck's Bad Boy,* this is a book that children never tire of reading or hearing. All the original familiar illustrations by W. H. Fry are included: 6 color plates, 18 black and white drawings. 159pp. 22345-0 Paperbound $2.00

MOTHER GOOSE MELODIES. Faithful republication of the fabulously rare Munroe and Francis "copyright 1833" Boston edition—the most important Mother Goose collection, usually referred to as the "original." Familiar rhymes plus many rare ones, with wonderful old woodcut illustrations. Edited by E. F. Bleiler. 128pp. 4½ x 6⅜. 22577-1 Paperbound $1.25

TWO LITTLE SAVAGES; BEING THE ADVENTURES OF TWO BOYS WHO LIVED AS INDIANS AND WHAT THEY LEARNED, Ernest Thompson Seton. Great classic of nature and boyhood provides a vast range of woodlore in most palatable form, a genuinely entertaining story. Two farm boys build a teepee in woods and live in it for a month, working out Indian solutions to living problems, star lore, birds and animals, plants, etc. 293 illustrations. vii + 286pp.

20985-7 Paperbound $2.50

PETER PIPER'S PRACTICAL PRINCIPLES OF PLAIN & PERFECT PRONUNCIATION. Alliterative jingles and tongue-twisters of surprising charm, that made their first appearance in America about 1830. Republished in full with the spirited woodcut illustrations from this earliest American edition. 32pp. $4\frac{1}{2}$ x $6\frac{3}{8}$.

22560-7 Paperbound $1.00

SCIENCE EXPERIMENTS AND AMUSEMENTS FOR CHILDREN, Charles Vivian. 73 easy experiments, requiring only materials found at home or easily available, such as candles, coins, steel wool, etc.; illustrate basic phenomena like vacuum, simple chemical reaction, etc. All safe. Modern, well-planned. Formerly *Science Games for Children*. 102 photos, numerous drawings. 96pp. $6\frac{1}{8}$ x $9\frac{1}{4}$.

21856-2 Paperbound $1.25

AN INTRODUCTION TO CHESS MOVES AND TACTICS SIMPLY EXPLAINED, Leonard Barden. Informal intermediate introduction, quite strong in explaining reasons for moves. Covers basic material, tactics, important openings, traps, positional play in middle game, end game. Attempts to isolate patterns and recurrent configurations. Formerly *Chess*. 58 figures. 102pp. (USO) 21210-6 Paperbound $1.25

LASKER'S MANUAL OF CHESS, Dr. Emanuel Lasker. Lasker was not only one of the five great World Champions, he was also one of the ablest expositors, theorists, and analysts. In many ways, his Manual, permeated with his philosophy of battle, filled with keen insights, is one of the greatest works ever written on chess. Filled with analyzed games by the great players. A single-volume library that will profit almost any chess player, beginner or master. 308 diagrams. xli x 349pp.

20640-8 Paperbound $2.75

THE MASTER BOOK OF MATHEMATICAL RECREATIONS, Fred Schuh. In opinion of many the finest work ever prepared on mathematical puzzles, stunts, recreations; exhaustively thorough explanations of mathematics involved, analysis of effects, citation of puzzles and games. Mathematics involved is elementary. Translated by F. Göbel. 194 figures. xxiv + 430pp. 22134-2 Paperbound $3.00

MATHEMATICS, MAGIC AND MYSTERY, Martin Gardner. Puzzle editor for Scientific American explains mathematics behind various mystifying tricks: card tricks, stage "mind reading," coin and match tricks, counting out games, geometric dissections, etc. Probability sets, theory of numbers clearly explained. Also provides more than 400 tricks, guaranteed to work, that you can do. 135 illustrations. xii + 176pp.

20338-2 Paperbound $1.50

PLANETS, STARS AND GALAXIES: DESCRIPTIVE ASTRONOMY FOR BEGINNERS, A. E. Fanning. Comprehensive introductory survey of astronomy: the sun, solar system, stars, galaxies, universe, cosmology; up-to-date, including quasars, radio stars, etc. Preface by Prof. Donald Menzel. 24pp. of photographs. 189pp. 5¼ x 8¼.
21680-2 Paperbound $1.50

TEACH YOURSELF CALCULUS, P. Abbott. With a good background in algebra and trig, you can teach yourself calculus with this book. Simple, straightforward introduction to functions of all kinds, integration, differentiation, series, etc. "Students who are beginning to study calculus method will derive great help from this book." Faraday House Journal. 308pp.
20683-1 Clothbound $2.00

TEACH YOURSELF TRIGONOMETRY, P. Abbott. Geometrical foundations, indices and logarithms, ratios, angles, circular measure, etc. are presented in this sound, easy-to-use text. Excellent for the beginner or as a brush up, this text carries the student through the solution of triangles. 204pp.
20682-3 Clothbound $2.00

TEACH YOURSELF ANATOMY, David LeVay. Accurate, inclusive, profusely illustrated account of structure, skeleton, abdomen, muscles, nervous system, glands, brain, reproductive organs, evolution. "Quite the best and most readable account,' *Medical Officer.* 12 color plates. 164 figures. 311pp. 4¾ x 7.
21651-9 Clothbound $2.50

TEACH YOURSELF PHYSIOLOGY, David LeVay. Anatomical, biochemical bases; digestive, nervous, endocrine systems; metabolism; respiration; muscle; excretion; temperature control; reproduction. "Good elementary exposition," *The Lancet.* 6 color plates. 44 illustrations. 208pp. 4¼ x 7.
21658-6 Clothbound $2.50

THE FRIENDLY STARS, Martha Evans Martin. Classic has taught naked-eye observation of stars, planets to hundreds of thousands, still not surpassed for charm, lucidity, adequacy. Completely updated by Professor Donald H. Menzel, Harvard Observatory. 25 illustrations. 16 x 30 chart. x + 147pp.
21099-5 Paperbound $1.25

MUSIC OF THE SPHERES: THE MATERIAL UNIVERSE FROM ATOM TO QUASAR, SIMPLY EXPLAINED, Guy Murchie. Extremely broad, brilliantly written popular account begins with the solar system and reaches to dividing line between matter and nonmatter; latest understandings presented with exceptional clarity. Volume One: Planets, stars, galaxies, cosmology, geology, celestial mechanics, latest astronomical discoveries; Volume Two: Matter, atoms, waves, radiation, relativity, chemical action, heat, nuclear energy, quantum theory, music, light, color, probability, antimatter, antigravity, and similar topics. 319 figures. 1967 (second) edition. Total of xx + 644pp.
21809-0, 21810-4 Two volumes, Paperbound $5.00

OLD-TIME SCHOOLS AND SCHOOL BOOKS, Clifton Johnson. Illustrations and rhymes from early primers, abundant quotations from early textbooks, many anecdotes of school life enliven this study of elementary schools from Puritans to middle 19th century. Introduction by Carl Withers. 234 illustrations. xxxiii + 381pp.
21031-6 Paperbound $2.50

MATHEMATICAL PUZZLES FOR BEGINNERS AND ENTHUSIASTS, Geoffrey Mott-Smith. 189 puzzles from easy to difficult—involving arithmetic, logic, algebra, properties of digits, probability, etc.—for enjoyment and mental stimulus. Explanation of mathematical principles behind the puzzles. 135 illustrations. viii + 248pp.
20198-8 Paperbound $1.75

PAPER FOLDING FOR BEGINNERS, William D. Murray and Francis J. Rigney. Easiest book on the market, clearest instructions on making interesting, beautiful origami. Sail boats, cups, roosters, frogs that move legs, bonbon boxes, standing birds, etc. 40 projects; more than 275 diagrams and photographs. 94pp.
20713-7 Paperbound $1.00

TRICKS AND GAMES ON THE POOL TABLE, Fred Herrmann. 79 tricks and games— some solitaires, some for two or more players, some competitive games—to entertain you between formal games. Mystifying shots and throws, unusual caroms, tricks involving such props as cork, coins, a hat, etc. Formerly *Fun on the Pool Table.* 77 figures. 95pp.
21814-7 Paperbound $1.00

HAND SHADOWS TO BE THROWN UPON THE WALL: A SERIES OF NOVEL AND AMUSING FIGURES FORMED BY THE HAND, Henry Bursill. Delightful picturebook from great-grandfather's day shows how to make 18 different hand shadows: a bird that flies, duck that quacks, dog that wags his tail, camel, goose, deer, boy, turtle, etc. Only book of its sort. vi + 33pp. 6½ x 9¼.   21779-5 Paperbound $1.00

WHITTLING AND WOODCARVING, E. J. Tangerman. 18th printing of best book on market. "If you can cut a potato you can carve" toys and puzzles, chains, chessmen, caricatures, masks, frames, woodcut blocks, surface patterns, much more. Information on tools, woods, techniques. Also goes into serious wood sculpture from Middle Ages to present, East and West. 464 photos, figures. x + 293pp.
20965-2 Paperbound $2.00

HISTORY OF PHILOSOPHY, Julián Marías. Possibly the clearest, most easily followed, best planned, most useful one-volume history of philosophy on the market; neither skimpy nor overfull. Full details on system of every major philosopher and dozens of less important thinkers from pre-Socratics up to Existentialism and later. Strong on many European figures usually omitted. Has gone through dozens of editions in Europe. 1966 edition, translated by Stanley Appelbaum and Clarence Strowbridge. xviii + 505pp. 21739-6 Paperbound $3.00

YOGA: A SCIENTIFIC EVALUATION, Kovoor T. Behanan. Scientific but non-technical study of physiological results of yoga exercises; done under auspices of Yale U. Relations to Indian thought, to psychoanalysis, etc. 16 photos. xxiii + 270pp.
20505-3 Paperbound $2.50

Prices subject to change without notice.
Available at your book dealer or write for free catalogue to Dept. GI, Dover Publications, Inc., 180 Varick St., N. Y., N. Y. 10014. Dover publishes more than 150 books each year on science, elementary and advanced mathematics, biology, music, art, literary history, social sciences and other areas.